The TEN COMMANDMENTS

Translated from Spanish by
Angie Torres Moure

DR. LES THOMPSON

Miami, Florida

LOGOI Ministries, established in 1968, is a mission organization created to be the *"place to go when Spanish pastors need help, advice and encouragement."* In keeping with this goal, a distance seminary was created that has graduated over 40,000 students. LOGOI's extensive online resource center is loaded with theological articles and materials specifically designed to help pastors and church leaders in their daily responsibilities. Along with these helps, LOGOI sponsors pastor conferences throughout the Spanish world, providing face-to-face help for Spanish leaders who haven't had an opportunity for formal Bible and theological training.

The Ten Commandments: Godly living in an ungodly world
© 2007 by the Rev. Leslie J. Thompson, Ph.D.

Unless noted, Scripture quotations are taken from the
Holy Bible, New Living Translation.
© 1996, 2004 Tyndale Charitable Trust
Used by permission of Tyndale House Publishers

Published by LOGOI Ministries
14540 SW 36th Street
Miami, FL 33186
www.logoi.org
Printed in Colombia, South America

ISBN 0-9705608-1-8

The author and publisher have sought to locate and secure permission to reprint copyright material in this book. If any such acknowledgments have been inadvertently omitted, the publisher would appreciate receiving the information so that proper credit may be given in future printings.

To my fourteen grandchildren
who have brought so much joy to my heart.

The Ten Commandments
have been theirs since childhood;
now as young adults
they strive to live according to these teachings.
May God bless each one to His glory.

ACKNOWLEDGMENTS

Some very special people made this book possible. First, Angie Torres Moure (my Spanish editorial assistant) kindly translated my *Los Diez Mandamientos* to English, making it possible for you to read it, too. That translated manuscript got into the capable hands of my son, Ed, who works beside me here at the ministry of LOGOI and served as editor. My wife Carolyn meticulously proofread, reviewed and corrected the copy. Once all my Spanish syntax was properly anglicized, a copy of the full manuscript was sent to Daniel, my preacher son (pastor of Christ Community Church in Titusville, Florida), who wrote the foreword. It was not the intention to make this a family project, but how pleased I am that this is what this book became! Finally, but not least, the cover and page design for the book was created by our LOGOI staff artist, Meredith Bozek. I owe a debt of gratitude to each with my heartfelt thanks.

TABLE OF CONTENTS

Editorial Note: The Catholic Church, following the textual divisions created by Saint Augustine, joins the first two commandments, calling it the First Commandment. Then, to reach ten, divides the last commandment in two. Most of the Catholic catechisms do not offer a full discussion of what many call the second commandment, that is, the making and adoring of images (see the English translation of the Catechism of the Catholic Church for the United States of America, copyright 1994, Paulist Press, Mahwah, New Jersey, and its brief argumentation for the use and veneration of images, pages 516 and 517).

Foreword

I first heard God's commandments from my father, whose book you hold in your hands. Around the kitchen table after dinner with the family, my dad would read the Bible. I had to listen, because he asked questions to make sure we were all paying attention. But I can honestly say that while my mind and body were there at the table, my heart wasn't! I could answer correctly when asked what God's commandments were. But I did not love God's law because I didn't understand it.

My sixteen-year-old daughter just received her driver's license. While we were out practicing her driving one afternoon, she said, "Dad, who decided all the speed limits must end with a zero or a five? Why not 51 or 23?" She was kidding, but she was also expressing something most of us believe: the laws by which we are forced to live are arbitrary things created by someone we don't know for reasons that don't make sense—they don't affect real life all that much.

For a long time that's how I thought about God's commandments. I thought God's laws were a list of arbitrary rules God chose just to see whether or not we would obey Him, rules that don't have much to do with life in the real world. It doesn't make a real practical difference in my life, I thought, if I have no other gods before God, or honor His name, or keep the Sabbath day holy, or refrain from coveting. In the

25 years I've served as a pastor, I've learned that most people think of God's law the same way I did.

We're taught as Christians to believe that God's law is good for many reasons: it reveals the character of God; it brings order and wisdom for life; it explains what it means to love God and to love our neighbors, it reveals our sin, convicts us of our guilt, and drives us to Christ to find a Savior. But we also discover the law is powerless. It can't give us righteousness. It can't set us free from our guilt or from sinful desires. Just knowing God says no to certain behavior doesn't give us the power or desire to do what God says. The law can't give life. It can't justify guilty people. The law doesn't save. Christ saves sinners. Law-keeping doesn't save anyone.

Because these things are true, we are prone to think, "If the law doesn't save, what's the point of keeping it?"

Honestly, when you read the Ten Commandments (and when you read the Sermon on the Mount and consider the deeper implications of God's commandments according to Jesus) do you think, "Wow, that's liberating! That's the path to real freedom and joy!" Probably not. It feels like God's law is a heavy burden. Law doesn't sound like good news because we don't understand its purposes!

At the beginning of human history, Adam and Eve believed two lies about God: that God's Word cannot be trusted, and that what God commands is not good. Satan's strategy hasn't changed. The battle we all fight on a daily basis is whether or not we will believe what God says and whether or not we will believe what He commands is good. I don't think any of us will find joy in obeying God until we're convinced God is wise and good in what He commands.

The battle I fight daily is to believe (not just intellectually, but to believe in my heart) that God's law is an expression of His love for me. God made me. He knows what is best for me. God is good and therefore He wants what is best for me. He commands what is in my best interest. His commands are not arbitrary rules intended just to test my willingness to obey. God's commands describe life as God intended it to be lived.

The gospel of God's grace in Christ Jesus is not just about being saved from the guilt and penalty of sin and escaping hell after I die. Jesus came to give life. The gospel is about living a new kind of life. God has delivered me from the dominion of darkness and transferred me into the Kingdom of His Son. He has set me free from the penalty my sin deserves. Jesus paid in full the debt I owe for my sin. But there's even more good news: God is setting me free from the controlling power of sin! The promise of the new covenant is that God writes His law on our hearts and gives us His Spirit. God is at work in us *"both to will and to do His good pleasure"* (Phil. 2:13).

Though salvation is by faith in Christ, not by our efforts at law-keeping, God's commandments continue to serve a good purpose. Through His commands, with all their implications, God shows us what it means for the bondage of sin to be broken in our lives. The more we believe God's law is wise and good, the more we will want to do what God says! Disobeying God doesn't set us free. Sin enslaves. Doing what God commands actually leads to the greatest joy and freedom!

While I believe God's commands express what is best for me, that doesn't mean I consistently do what God commands. God's commands probe my heart deeply, revealing desires and attitudes, thoughts and intentions that are sinful. It's God's grace at work in me that enables me—progressively, often gradually, but inevitably— to see the truth about the sin deep inside.

I have to see the truth about my sin before change is possible. I have to hate my sin before I will run from it. And I won't see my sin for what it is without a growing knowledge of God's commandments. Thus God's work in my life is inseparably tied to His law. It's God's grace at work in me that teaches me to see sinful desires for what they are, that changes my heart so I will say no to those desires, and that defines what it means to live a godly life in Christ Jesus. I can't know what it means to live right before God without God's commandments! Understanding the multifaceted implications of God's commandments is vitally relevant to daily life.

There's one more aspect to the good news of the gospel as it relates to the law of God: What happens when we fail to do what God says? I am afraid too many Christians live with the idea that bad things that happen are a form of punishment for some act of disobedience to God's commandments. They assume they are blessed by God when everything goes smoothly and there are no problems. When problems or pain come along, they assume they're experiencing God's punishment for some specific sin they've committed.

There's a family in the church I serve whose son is in trouble with the law for doing something stupid. These parents have beat themselves up trying to figure out what they did wrong that has brought about this experience of God's punishment. I have tried to convince them that what is happening may have nothing to do with anything they did, good or bad. Certainly there are mistakes they've made. Christian parents are still sinners. But their son made his own choices. They did not condition him to behave as he did, though certain patterns in their home may have made it easier for him to choose as he did.

Rather than punishment, it may be God's blessing and goodness to their son that has brought this young man to this point of having to face some things in his own heart. In love, God may be working to set him free from patterns that could have become much more destructive if left uncorrected.

I believe it radically changes the way we respond

to pain, suffering and hardship, if we learn to believe that God has already punished Jesus for our sin. Whatever difficult circumstances God brings into our lives are part of God's loving work, intended for good purposes: "...*you know that the testing of your faith develops perseverance. Perseverance must finish its work so that you may be mature and complete, not lacking anything*" (James 1:3-4).

If we believe the message of the Bible, we have to conclude that God does not punish us for our sin. He may chastise or correct when we persist in sin (not necessarily by sending painful circumstances, He can correct in less severe ways). The fact is, God doesn't punish us for our sin if we belong to Christ Jesus. That's the message in the book of Job. There is not a one-to-one relationship between our sin and the hardship or suffering we experience. God does not zap you when you disobey His commands. He is patient and longsuffering, slow to anger and abounding in lovingkindness. As the psalmist says, "*He does not treat us as our sins deserve or repay us according to our iniquity*" (Psalm 103:10).

God punished Jesus for our sin. The penalty we deserve was paid in full by Jesus on the cross. For God to punish us for sin that Jesus was already punished for would be unjust, and God is never unjust. God may correct and chasten us as a loving father disciplines His children. He may use adversity to show us the danger of our sin and leads us away from it. But even in that kind of severity, God always acts in love toward His children! In all He brings into our lives, He is working for our ultimate good. That's the essence of love—love always desires the best for the beloved.

As you read through the chapters of this book, may God use it to lead you to echo the psalmist: *"Happy are people of integrity, who follow the law of the Lord. Happy are those who obey His decrees and search for Him with all their hearts"* (Psalm 119:1,2). I'm convinced this short study of the Ten Commandments will further your understanding of how God's Law affects every aspect of our lives. The law of God is not in conflict with the Gospel of grace. It is intensely practical. Read the book. Think about the implications of God's commandments. And ask God to give you the grace to believe that what He commands is wise and good!

Dan Thompson

INTRODUCTION

WHY do we need the Ten Commandments? We live in a world where people choose what they want to do as well as what they want to believe. What matters most is what's personally pleasing, convenient and satisfying. No one wants laws or rules. We don't like restrictions of any kind. Our goal is to be free to do whatever we please without anyone's interference.

Furthermore, we're not all that fussy about our beliefs—whether they're true or false—as long as they're convenient. What matters most is to be free to live life according to our liking.

The problem most of us have with the Ten Commandments is that they get in our face. God tells us what we shouldn't do, as well as what we should do. Such prohibitions and demands go against our grain. So, the easiest thing is to toss out the Ten Commandments with the explanation that we live by grace and not by law, or that these commandments were given to a people of another time and with other problems. Or even that the Commandments are no longer relevant.

God allows people to choose what they want to do.

God, however, puts these laws out front and center for all peoples, no matter who they are or where they live. No one can simply make them disappear without running counter to God Himself.

It's not that He stuffs each one of these commands down people's throats. God simply allows people to see as well as to experience the consequences of not following His rules. When people choose to disregard His laws, they simply come apart at the seams. Respect for others is lost, horrific murders occur, sexual and sadistic crimes take place, possessions are no longer safe, truth flies out the window, greed and corruption become the norm, not to mention the kind of godlessness people fall into.

Most certainly, God allows people to choose what they want to do. He rarely, if ever, interferes with a person's free will. But that's where people take a stand, with their personal desire on one side and God's commands on the other. They make their choices, much like the challenge Joshua put before the Israelites:

> ...if you refuse to serve the LORD, then choose today whom you will serve. Would you prefer the gods your ancestors served beyond the Euphrates [that is, the gods of the Egyptians]? Or will it be the gods of the Amorites [the gods served by their pagan neighbors] in whose land you now live? But as for me and my family, [said Joshua] we will serve the LORD (Joshua 24:15).

Since no area of life is left out in God's Ten Commandments, the way we live—our relationships, our children, our work, our service to God and community—is affected. That's how very important each commandment is. That's why we need to learn all we can about each one.

Let's look at the New Testament. What advice are we given in reference to God's commandments? We see that in Romans 2:14-16 non-Jews are also mentioned in connection with God's Law:

> Even when Gentiles, who do not have God's written law, instinctively follow what the law says, they show that in their hearts they know right from wrong. They demonstrate that God's law is written within them, for their own consciences either accuse them or tell them they are doing what is right. The day will surely come when God, by Jesus Christ, will judge everyone's secret life. This is my message.

Our behavior is so important to God that He's put special "genes" in all of us so that from birth we're able to differentiate good from bad. This God-given conscience accuses us when we do wrong, and it affirms us when we do what's right. Good though that is, it's not enough. What ultimately defines the good and the bad, what guides us conclusively as to what's right and what's wrong are the Ten Commandments. That's where we get the detail.

What guides us as to what's right and what's wrong are the Ten Commandments

Here's another indicator given us by Jesus Himself as to the applicability of His laws in our day and His desire that we obey them:

> *Don't misunderstand why I have come. I did not come to abolish the law of Moses or the writings of the prophets. No, I came to accomplish their purpose. I tell you the truth, until heaven and earth disappear, not even the smallest detail of God's law will disappear until its purpose is achieved. So if you ignore the least command-ment and teach others to do the same, you will be called the least in the Kingdom of Heaven. But anyone who obeys God's laws and teaches them will be called great in the Kingdom of Heaven* (Matthew 5:17-19).

God's laws haven't changed. His commandments are just as valid today as they were the first time the ancient Israelites received them (see Galatians 5:19-21, Ephesians 5:2-6; Colossians 3:5-9). Paul tells us that without these commandments he wouldn't have known how to behave:

> *...it was the law that showed me my sin. I would never have known that coveting is wrong if the law had not said, "You must not covet." But sin used this command to arouse all kinds of covetous desires within me! If there were no law, sin would not have that power. At one time I lived without understanding the law. But when I learned the command not to covet, for instance, the power of sin came to life, and I died. So I discovered that the law's commands,*

which were supposed to bring life, brought
spiritual death instead. Sin took advantage of
those commands and deceived me; it used the
commands to kill me. But still, the law itself is
holy, and its commands are holy and right and
good (Romans 7:7-12).

Possibly you've picked up this book out of curiosity. Now that you've read the introduction, how about taking a few moments to glance through the rest of the book? Do you see any items of interest? Are there any subjects that might be helpful to you?

In each chapter you'll notice that the subject matter talks about a loving God who blesses and cares for His children. And that care and concern come as a result of obedience to His requirements. That's what makes every commandment important. Not one area of our human existence is left out. Let me be quick to add that not one of us is capable of fully obeying all of these requirements. At the same time, we'll discover that God has promised each one of us His gracious and divine help. It's possible to live life in a way that pleases God.

This book won't provide an exhaustive study of the Commandments. My hope, however, is that the succinct, clear and modern-day explanation given for each Commandment will motivate each one of us to want to truly walk in a godly manner in this ungodly world.

THE TEN COMMANDMENTS
Exodus 20:1-17

(In Deuteronomy 5:5-21 the Ten Commandments are repeated.) All Scripture quotations used in this book are taken from The New Living Translation.

"Then God gave the people all these instructions: "I am the LORD your God, who rescued you from the land of Egypt, the place of your slavery.

1. *You must not have any other god but me.*
2. *You must not make for yourself an idol of any kind or an image of anything in the heavens or on the earth or in the sea. You must not bow down to them or worship them, for I, the LORD your God, am a jealous God who will not tolerate your affection for any other gods. I lay the sins of the parents upon their children; the entire family is affected—even children in the third and fourth generations of those who reject me. But I lavish unfailing love for a thousand generations on those who love me and obey my commands.*
3. *You must not misuse the name of the LORD your God. The LORD will not let you go unpunished if you misuse his name.*
4. *Remember to observe the Sabbath day by keeping it holy. You have six days each week for your ordinary work, but the seventh day is a Sabbath day of rest dedicated to the LORD your God. On that day no one*

in your household may do any work. This includes you, your sons and daughters, your male and female servants, your livestock, and any foreigners living among you. For in six days the LORD made the heavens, the earth, the sea, and everything in them; but on the seventh day he rested. That is why the LORD blessed the Sabbath day and set it apart as holy.

5. Honor your father and mother. Then you will live a long, full life in the land the LORD your God is giving you.

6. You must not murder.

7. You must not commit adultery.

8. You must not steal.

9. You must not testify falsely against your neighbor.

10. You must not covet your neighbor's house. You must not covet your neighbor's wife, male or female servant, ox or donkey, or anything else that belongs to your neighbor."

THE FIRST COMMANDMENT

You must not have any other god but me (Exodus 20:3).

**Are non-Christians the only ones who
bow down to false gods?**

**Are you sure the god you worship
is the God of the Bible?**

**What are some of the special gods
we need to disown?**

THERE'S no doubt about it, we're all prone to idolatry. There are things we love, seek, and wish for that, if we're not careful, we'll worship as if they were God. We tend to give these specially chosen idols all our energy, time and money. They become our little (or big) god and our substitute for the true and living God.

When I was a teenager growing up in Cuba I was crazy about a girl. We lived on a farm outside the town limits of Placetas, and the only female friends I had were my mother and my sister. This girl I had a crush on worked at a pharmacy, on the north corner of the central plaza in town. Every chance I got I would bicycle around to the pharmacy to see if she was there. Now, I need you to understand that I was terribly shy. I'd never spoken a word to her. I didn't even know her name. But that didn't matter. See-ing her filled me with happiness. For days my imagination filled with the thought of her, and I'd walk on the clouds. Nothing else on earth mattered; in my mind I was totally devoted to that name-less, pretty-faced girl.

Imagined gods end up as substitutes for the Almighty.

A few years later, my parents sent me to Canada—to my grandmother's—to continue my studies. There I made friends with a fellow student who had a passion for cars. For him it was more than mere excitement. When he saw a new car he immediately insisted on opening the hood to "ooh" and "ahh" about the engine. He'd spend most of his time and all his money on cars and car parts. He pampered them, dreamed about them, and lived for them. He was happiest when he was in a garage with his arms covered with grease, his hands snaked around a motor, and his fingers firmly grasping a tool. His love for cars was plastered in photos all over the walls of his bedroom.

Could the First Commandment possibly refer to such things—a childhood crush, passion for cars? What about a passion for sports, clothing, sex, money and such like? And, coming right to the point, what is an idol anyway? We need guidelines.

To find an accurate definition let's turn to the Bible. Idols, we'll discover, fall into three categories:

1. *Any object that is considered supernatural and worshipped as god is considered an idol, and directly forbidden by this commandment. We find such "gods" in many of the ancient religions of the Egyptians, Greeks and Romans. Obviously, those imagined gods end up as substitutes for the Almighty:*

   It's interesting to see that people worshipped the sun, the moon, the stars, air, fire, water, rocks, hills, even certain plants, trees and animals. In fact, some of these same objects are worshipped by people in the New Age movement. This adoration of imagined supernatural objects is strictly prohibited by the First Commandment. Also forbidden is the worship of men who claim to be god; for example, King Darius described in the sixth chapter of the Book of Daniel. In Miami we have a man, Jose Luis de Jesus de Miranda, who claims to be Jesus and says that someday he will rule the world. Add to this the list of countless dead saints to whom some people pray believing they have supernatural powers. All such adoration is prohibited by this First Commandment (Exodus 20:4; Leviticus 26:1; Deuteronomy 7:25; 11:16; Isaiah 42:8; 1 John 5:21; Romans 1:22-25; Psalm 115:4-8).

2. *An idol or a god can also be something material—something that absorbs all our interest, something to which we devote all our energy. When something becomes the all important driving force in our lives—that to which we devote our time, money and heart— we've created an idol.*

   Thus, an idol can be money, fame, power, pleasure, family, intellect, sex, beauty, fashion, popularity, sports, recognition, or any number of similar things. Even though that which we passionately adore can be good and honorable in and of itself, when it absorbs all our interest, time, heart and fantasy it becomes our god. The First Commandment forbids it (1Corinthians 8:5; Acts 17:29; Philippians 3:19; Romans 1:21-26; Luke 16:13; Ephesians 5:5). In this connection read some of the verses that describe God's great love for us. They state He loves us so passionately that He gets jealous when we adore and worship other things beside Him (Exodus 34:14; Deuteronomy 4:24; 6:15, Joshua 24:19; 2Kings 17:15; 1John 2:15-17; James 4:4; 2Timothy 4:10).

3. *This First Commandment also prohibits the adoration of supernatural evil spirits (Satan and his demons) that seek to be worshipped and served as if they were God.*

   This type of idolatry encompasses the direct as well as indirect worship of Satan. Such worship can occur through such means as spiritism, witchcraft, Santeria, fortune telling, Ouija boards, séances, tarot cards, horoscopes, palm reading, good luck charms and anything to do with so-called "spirit guides." All of these depend directly or indirectly on powers related to Satan who, as a supernatural being, tries to manifest himself as if he were a god himself. The most detailed prohibition regarding the worship of Satan and

An idol is anything that replaces the one, true, and living God.

demons is found in Deuteronomy 18:10-14; Exodus 22:18; Leviticus 19:31; 20:6; 1Samuel 15:23; 28:7; 2Kings 17:17; 23:24; 1Chronicles 10:13; Isaiah 8:19; Ezekiel 13:23; Micah 5:12; Galatians 5:20; Revelation 21:8.

In summary, we can say that an idol is anything that takes the place of the one, true, and living God described and revealed in the Bible. He demands that we serve and worship Him alone.

Power Evangelism

Not everyone agrees with these definitions. Rather recently a school of thought called Power Evangelism has developed in Latin America that especially objects to our first and second definition. They accept only the third one. They've decided that the First Commandment deals exclusively with the worship of Satan and his demons.[1]

I strongly disagree with such a narrow definition. For example, in Romans 1:23 Paul tells us that people create all kinds of gods. He says these are made *"to look like mere people, or birds and animals and snakes."* He makes no reference to Satan, spirits, or demons. Furthermore, in his letter to the Philippians he speaks of those *"whose god is their appetite"*—again, making no association with Satan or the supernatural. Similarly, in James 4:4 we read that *"friendship with this world,"* which doesn't necessarily include Satan, can substitute for the worship of God. Further, Paul explains that Demas deserted him *"because he loves the things of this life"* (2Timothy 4:10); he doesn't say Demas loved Satan. I believe this First Commandment deals with anything that takes God's rightful place in our lives, not exclusively the worship of Satan and his demons.

> *Why would anyone try and redo what Christ has already done so magnificently?*

Nonetheless, these groups in Latin America have grown so strong and influential that many have come to accept their conclusions. They believe that the big force and opposition to God is the devil and his demons and all non-Christians are shackled and fettered by Satan. In order for the non-Christians to believe in Christ they first must be freed. Accordingly, Christians

[1] See *Hard-Core Idolatry: Facing the Facts* by Peter Wagner, Wagner Publications, Colorado Springs, Co. 1999.

must declare open war on Satan and all the human host who worship him. For this battle the Power Evangelists have developed new and novel devices (not found in the Bible): prayer chains, marches for Jesus, prayer walks, all night vigils, purification bonfires, and a number of special techniques for binding demons. According to their beliefs, these methods set entire cities, communities, and even nations free from the power and grasp of Satan. Thus loosed, people can turn from Satan to Christ.

What does the Bible say? Can we, by our human actions and methods, set people free so that they can be saved? Hasn't Christ already done this? Neither in the gospels nor in Acts of the Apostles—nor anywhere else in the Bible, for that matter—do we have an instance where Christians approached evangelism by first challenging and expelling demons. It would appear these modern groups are trying to repeat—inadequately at best—what Christ has already done through his death and resurrection. Paul in Colossians 1:13 teaches that Christ has already gloriously *"rescued us from the one who rules in the kingdom of darkness"* and brought us *"into the Kingdom of his dear Son."* Why would anyone try and redo what Christ has already done so magnificently?

At the same time, I'm very much aware that Satan is alive, although I would question whether he's as capable and powerful as some people infer. Because Christ at Calvary won that all-important cosmic battle,

Satan has been defeated. We should give Satan no more credit than the little he deserves. In fact, we must count on the fact that he has been eternally defeated and that Christ is the victor! That's the reason Paul can tell us Satan's temptations don't need to overwhelm us: *"Remember that the temptations that come into your life are no different from what others experience. And God is faithful. He will keep the temptation from becoming so strong that you can't stand up against it. When you are tempted, he will show you a way out so that you will not give in to it"* (1Corinthians 10:13). Christ is the one in control. He alone deserves our adoration and worship.

An illustration of love for God

The more we study the First Commandment the more we realize that our real struggle is not with Satan but with our own desires and affections. My dad, Elmer Thompson, often recounted his personal struggle between love for God and material things.

One Sunday afternoon—August of 1922—as a twenty-one year-old, he climbed a hill behind his parents' home. He wanted one more look at the farm that spread out through the valley. For several years he'd worked that land, growing corn and beans, raising a few head of cattle, and earning enough to buy a car. Lately, he'd been thinking about giving that all up to go to Bible college and serve God full time.

From his post on the hill he could clearly see Pike's Peak off in the west toward the Colorado Rockies.

Looking east, he could count his calves, see the cows he milked, the rows of corn and the patch of string beans he'd planted. As he looked at that stretch of land, he realized he loved it. Before climbing the hill he'd re-read the contract his father had so generously prepared. All he needed to do was sign it and that farm was his. He was well aware that owning a farm close to Denver would make anyone proud, possibly even wealthy.

Our real struggle is not with Satan but with our own desires and affections

But something deep inside held him back. He somehow sensed God had something other than a farm in his future, a sense he couldn't get rid of. At the same time, going off to Bible college scared him—his hands were used to milking cows, not writing sermons; wrestling cows, not reading books. However, he'd learned from his dad that the most important thing in life was doing what God wanted him to do. Before climbing the hill that morning he had prayed: *"Not my will, but Thine be done."*

As the sun began to set over the Rockies, shadows like long fingers seemed to stretch out toward him as if reaching for his heart. He had to decide, but what? Was it wrong to want a farm? Should he throw that dream away? Was it really God who was calling him to go to Bible college? What would he do, where would he go? While he loved the farm, he simply wasn't comfortable with that choice. Now he could no longer put off the decision. He'd promised his dad he would come down the hill with an answer.

He took one last look. The corn waved happily in the breeze. The cows chewed their cuds contentedly. The calves nudged their mothers for milk. From that distance he could hear his horse bray. Was it asking him to hurry up his decision? The question that dug deep—that had bothered him all day—again bombarded his mind. Did he love the farm more than he loved God? With a swing of determination he turned his back on the beautiful scene below. And falling on his knees cried out, "Lord, you know how difficult this decision is for me, but as I've promised you, I want your will, not mine. Right here on this hill I give you my heart and all that I am. Here's my life, do what you want with me."

God doesn't come to take away the very things He has created for us to enjoy.

Five years later, January 12, 1927, Elmer Thompson was once again climbing. This time it was onto a ship, *the Pacific and Orient Lines*. His destiny was Cuba. The farm in Colorado was a faded memory. His heart now burned with a desire to teach young Cuban men and women the Word of God. Like Abraham, he had left his land, his father's household, and all he knew. He had traded a farm for the mission field.

He was to discover that Jesus' promise would prove true: *"Everyone who has given up houses or brothers or* sisters or father or mother or children or property, for my sake, will receive a hundred times as much in return and will have eternal life" (Matthew 19:29). Twenty years later there were hundreds of churches all over central Cuba,[2] plus hundreds more throughout the Caribbean Islands, giving testimony to what God could do with a young man who put his love for God above earthly things.

A mistaken interpretation

We could easily misunderstand what God wants to tell us when He says: "You must not have any other god but me." We could mistakenly think God wants to take away everything we love. Or, that we should never want success, or fame, or money because such things could so easily become our false gods. Following that line of thought, we could conclude that to be saintly and pious we should never strive for much of anything, or we'll become idolaters.

That would be an altogether mistaken conclusion. God doesn't come to take away the very things He has created for us to enjoy. He's not a sadist. He made us material beings—that's why material things appeal to us. And He made all kinds of things for us to enjoy, because He wants us to be happy. Jesus said: "My purpose is to give [my followers] a rich and satisfying life" (John 10:10).

Therefore, we must understand clearly what it is He asks of us in this commandment. Clearly, we're not to desire anything more than we desire God. That's it!

---

[2] God used my father to establish The West Indies Mission, now called World Team.

Nothing more than God! Furthermore, because He created us, He knows we are happiest when we live life the way He planned it. When we obey His laws, when we refuse to let unworthy gods steal our affections, then—and only then—we are happiest.

The rights God claims for Himself

What right does God have to tell us, *"You shall have no other gods before Me?"* In the preface to this commandment we find the answer: *"I am the LORD your God, who brought you out of the land of Egypt, out of the house of slavery."* God is a God who delivers us from bondage. As He liberated the Israelites from the hand of Pharaoh and set them free, so He has liberated us from the slavery of sin, and provided us eternal salvation. David in one of his psalms explains the joy of this liberation:

> *The LORD heard my cry. He lifted me out of the pit of despair, out of the mud and the mire. He set my feet on solid ground and... has given me a new song to sing...* (Psalm 40:1-3).

It's the message proclaimed in the gospel:

> *You do not belong to yourself, for God bought you with a high price. So you must honor God with your body* (1Corinthians 6:19-20).

The cross on which Jesus spilled His blood because of His great love for mankind is proof enough. The death He died gave Him the right to make the demand: *"You must not have any other god but me."* To worship other gods is to belittle all that God is. It's to belittle all Jesus did to redeem us and reconcile us to God the Father.

There's one final thing that needs mentioning. Since we're required to love God with all our heart, soul and mind, how can we love Him if we don't really know Him? We love somebody

God has liberated us from the slavery of sin, and provided us eternal salvation.

when we know that person and appreciate all he/she is, has, and does. When we really get to know such a person, when we experience the great love that person has for us, then we can respond in kind.

What's God like? How can we get to know Him? Surely, if we're serious about obeying this commandment, we'll want to know God and take whatever steps are necessary to get to know Him.

That means the Bible will become a book we'll want to read over and over again. Also, we'll discover there are many godly men who've written wonderful books about what they've learned about God. We'll ask a pastor or friends for recommendations. We'll buy some of these books. We'll study them and learn all we can about God. We'll fall in love with God—I guarantee it! The result will be that we'll want to obey this First Commandment.

THE SECOND COMMANDMENT

You must not make for yourself an idol of any kind or an image of anything in the heavens or on the earth or in the sea. You must not bow down to them or worship them, for I, the LORD your God, am a jealous God who will not tolerate your affection for any other gods. I lay the sins of the parents upon their children; the entire family is affected— even children in the third and fourth generations of those who reject me. But I lavish unfailing love for a thousand generations on those who love me and obey my commands (Exodus 20:4-6).

Have you ever thought about the way
you worship God?

Could it be that you're not worshiping
Him correctly?

What does the Bible teach us?

WHILE the first commandment limits our worship to the only true God, the second commandment tells us how He wants to be worshipped. The problem we have is our tendency to worship God the way we want to, rather than the way He wants us to.

I have always had a vivid imagination. To this day that imagination can cause many sleepless nights. Sometimes I wish I had a key I could turn off in my brain so I could get some sleep. I clearly remember a sleepless night when as a boy I tried to imagine what God was like. For our evening devotions Dad read us the story of Moses and the burning bush. That night again and again I relived that scene. I watched as Moses walked over to the bush in the fields. I noticed how startled he was when the voice spoke to him out of the bush. Those words rang in my ears: *"Moses, Moses, take off your shoes. The ground where you are walking is holy."*

> *Our tendency is to worship God the way we want to, rather than the way He wants us to.*

There on my pillow I peered out into the dark Cuban night. I imagined the tree outside my window catching fire. I imagined a voice calling out from it: "Les, Les, this is God speaking." The thought made me uncomfortable. Then my mind began churning. What if God did come to my window? What if He did talk to me? No, I reasoned, He doesn't do that kind of thing anymore. Anyway, He wouldn't come to my window.

Mother, the day before, had told me she did not think I was a Christian because of the things I was doing. God visits good people, not bad, so I was safe, I thought.

I tried to push God out of mind. He was way off in heaven, too far away to be interested in me. That night I convinced myself God was beyond the most distant stars, too far away and far too busy to be interested in anything I was doing. Arriving at that satisfying conclusion, I hid my head under the sheets and fell asleep.

Years later, when in Bible college, I learned I had reached a conclusion similar to that of Immanuel Kant (1724-1804): "God exists in another sphere. There is no way He can communicate with us or us with Him." Such ideas may salve our conscience and perhaps let us sleep at night, but such twisted concepts of God lead us to false worship, to a god we have created in our own minds and not to the God of the Bible.

Even later, when I became a serious student of God's Word, I realized how mistaken my ideas had been. I learned how important it is to worship the true God, the way the Bible presents Him from Genesis to Revelation.

Our concepts of God

What we know about God, His character, His attributes, His ways and His relationship to us is found exclusively in the Bible. How do we see our God? Do we accept what the Bible says about Him and about us, or do we try to change God and recreate Him into a god more to our liking? Let me give some examples.

- New "translations" of the Bible —stuffed with gender inclusive language—have been made in a deliberate attempt to remove its masculinity. You may ask, "What's the big deal?" For one thing, we expect translations of the Bible to be as faithful as possible to the original text. Secondly, it can't be right for translators to arbitrarily remove all the male pronouns—like "he" and "him," along with other male terms—especially when the original language is gender specific. On the surface such changes may appear harmless, until we consider how these changes may alter our understanding of the Bible. We must beware of any Bible version that purposefully seeks to change our concept of God, what He is like, and what He has told us about humankind.

- Similarly, those who seek to make homosexuality acceptable deliberately try to change the character of God. They try to make Him a loving, non-condemning, permissive God. They refuse to take at face value what the Bible says about their lifestyle and about the nature of God, and make Him into something the Bible in no way supports.

- Genesis chapter 4 tells the story of Cain. He, too, thought God was a tolerant, easy to please God, indifferent to the ways we worship Him. When it came his turn to offer a sacrifice, he picked fruit from his garden and offered it to Him. But we read that God *"did not accept Cain and his offering."* Clearly, Cain was totally mistaken about the way he visualized God.

- Leviticus 10 tells the story of the sons of Aaron, Nadab and Abihu. They decided to be creative, and brought the Lord *"a different fire than he had commanded."* God killed them instantly. Their false concept of what God was like and what He demanded caused their deaths.

We try to reconstruct God to make Him into a more agreeable god.

These are just a few of countless examples of the many ways we try to reconstruct God to make Him into a more agreeable god, one more to our liking. This is exactly what Paul tells us in Romans 1:21-23: *"They knew God, but they wouldn't worship him as God or even give him thanks. And they began to think up foolish ideas of what God was like. The result was that their minds became dark and confused. Claiming to be wise, they became utter fools instead. And instead of worshiping the glorious, ever-living God, they worshiped idols…"*

Our amazing imagination

Back in 1748 a Frenchman, Julien Offray de la Mettrie, said: "By the imagination, by its flattering brush, the cold skeleton of reason takes on living and ruddy flesh, by the imagination the sciences flourish, the arts are adorned, the wood speaks, the echoes sigh, the rocks weep, marble breathes, and all inanimate objects gain life… It reasons, judges, analyzes, compares, and investigates." What an amazing and powerful instrument each of us has!

Michelangelo's, Picasso's, Goya's, and Del Greco's imaginations made them the amazing artists they became. Imagination also made Galileo, Madam Curie, and Einstein great scientists. Through their imagination Adam Smith, Karl Marx, and John Keynes set standards in the world's economy. Great imaginations produced the kind of writing Shakespeare, Hemingway, and Robert Frost gave us. The imaginations of John Adams, Winston Churchill, and Charles de Gaulle gave us great politicians. The imaginations of Martin Luther, John Wesley and Billy Graham set the religious world on fire.

When our minds choose what God wants instead of what we want, our minds are transformed by Him.

On the other hand, it is also the great power of the imagination that drags so many down the horrible path of pornography, the occult, murder and countless other evils. In truth, we become what we think! This is the reason Paul calls us to be transformed *"by changing the way we think."* This takes place, according to him, when our bodies become *"a living and holy* sacrifice—*the kind God will accept."* When our minds choose what God wants instead of what we want, our minds are transformed by Him. Then we will see *"what God wants us to do, and we will know how good and pleasing and perfect his will really is"* (Romans 12:1-2).

What does God really want?

Recently I saw a TV program featuring the notorious NBA basketball player Dennis Rodman. Between 1990 and 1998 he led the National Basketball Association in rebounds and was a key player in the Chicago Bulls Championship seasons. That, however, wasn't what Dennis lived for. According to the program, he had an insatiable sexual appetite, one that eventually led him down a path that not only ended his career, but made him lose the respect of those who had previously admired him. It saddened me to see how his choices led him down such a pitiful and lonely path.

Like Rodman, we all tend to serve what we love. If we do not suppress our sinful appetites, they too, will destroy us. That's why the God who knows us so well commands us:

> *You must not make for yourself an idol of any kind or an image of anything in the heavens or on the earth or in the sea. You must not bow down to them or worship them, for I, the LORD your God, am a jealous God who will not tolerate your affection for any other gods. I lay the sins of the parents upon their children; the entire family is*

affected—even children in the third and fourth
generations of those who reject me…

With this command, He gave us four reasons to obey Him: 1) He is the Lord our God; 2) He is all powerful; 3) He is jealous; 4) He punishes sins.

First, he reminds us of who He is. He uses His name "YHWH." Each letter in His name is the first letter of the Hebrew words for "was," "is," and "will be." He is the unchanging God, who remains the same yesterday, today, and forever. As we know, there is no known pronunciation for YHWH. And that is as it should be: our God is simply beyond comparison, inexplicably glorious, sublimely majestic. As the Supreme Being, He demands we adore him beyond any other love, appetite or desire.

Second, God reminds us He is omnipotent. When in our imagination we try to reduce Him to fit our little "box," we totally distort Him and rob Him of His omnipotence. In doing so, we make Him a fragile, weak, and limited being. When, as the Apostle Paul says in Romans 1:23, people imagine Him to be a bird, a lizard or a beetle, they no longer need to fear Him. In fact, people try to make Him so insignificant and powerless they actually believe they can control and manipulate Him. This is why Isaiah asks, *"To whom, then, can we compare God? What image might we find to resemble him"* (40:18)? Then he delivers the answer from YHWH Himself: *"I am God--I alone! I am God, and there is no one else like me. Only I can tell you what is going to happen even before it happens. Everything I plan will come to pass, for I do whatever I wish"* (46:9-11).

Third, God tells us He is a jealous God. This is a characteristic we find hard to accept. We don't like arrogant, self-centered, jealous people. Actually, most consider jealousy a terrible vice. To think of God as "jealous," then, needs explanation. Perhaps we can better understand Him when we think of family. As a husband, I certainly don't want to see my wife in another man's arms, nor do I want to have someone else try to replace me as Dad to my children. I am extremely jealous of their love and affection. Likewise, when God speaks of His jealousy, He is describing His love for us. He wants nothing to come between us. He wants no other love to steal away our affection for Him. This was the same kind of jealousy that moved Jesus when He cried over Jerusalem: *"O Jerusalem, Jerusalem, you who kill the prophets and stone God's messengers! How often I have wanted to gather your children together as a hen protects her chicks beneath her wings, but you wouldn't let me"* (Matthew 23:37).

> *God wants no other love to steal away our affection for Him.*

Lastly, God warns against worshipping false gods. He says: *"I punish the children for the sins of their parents to the third and fourth generations. But I lavish my love on those who love me and obey my commands, even for a thousand generations*" (Exodus 34:7). Some have suggested that these words refer to curses (in some cases demons) that move from parents to children, often called "generational curses." A proponent, Don Rogers, states: "Generational curses are judgments that are passed on to individuals because of sins perpetuated in a family in a number of generations…"

I disagree. I see no reference to curses or demons in the statement. Rather, I believe this passage refers to a far more obvious conclusion. To say it succinctly, there are direct consequences for deliberate disobedience. When parents refuse to obey God, to respect or love Him; when they choose to serve and worship false gods, there is direct, long-range fallout on their children, unless God intervenes. Without parents as spiritual guides, children are prone to make horrible spiritual choices. Poor parental choices can affect families for generations, keeping children and grand-children from loving and serving God. How carefully God has sought to guard family life so that children have the opportunity to love and serve Him.

We read: *"Then as the LORD finished speaking with Moses on Mount Sinai, he gave him the two stone tablets inscribed with the terms of the covenant, written by the finger of God"* (Exodus 31:18). This is one of very few instances in the Bible where words were written by the finger of God. There is only one other statement like this one in the Bible, when King Belshazzar saw the hand of God write on the wall, as described in Daniel

5. Both writings describe the critical importance of what God is saying to man. To deliberately ignore these God-given words is to literally turn our backs on Him. To choose a lifestyle in disobedience to this commandment dishonors God. The results can only be disastrous for every member of the family, as well as for the extended family. Even so, there is hope!

A continuation of promised mercies

God's command doesn't end on a negative note. He says: *"I lavish unfailing love for a thousand generations on those who love me and obey my commands"* (Exodus 20:6). And I have first-hand evidence of that love lavished for generations on our family.

My mom comes from a long line of Christian Scotts, dating all the way back to the time John Knox set Scotland on fire for God in the mid 1500s. Preachers, pastors and missionaries are scattered throughout our ancestral line. Eight of my grandmother's children served as missionaries. At one time my grandmother McElheran had a child serving on every continent except Australia. My mother went to Cuba and with my father started the West Indies Mission (now World Team). All six of us children were born and raised in Cuba. Later, all of us served as missionaries (except for a sister who suffered from multiple sclerosis).

Without parents as spiritual guides, children are prone to make horrible spiritual choices.

My older sister went to Brazil; a brother served in Cuba, another in Spain and the Dominican Republic, another sister served in Haiti, and I have spent my life serving first in Cuba and then throughout Latin America.

God blesses families who love Him and heed His commandments.

God's mercy and goodness haven't stopped there. My wife and I are blessed with four sons. All four are serving the Lord full time. Now we're watching to see how the Lord will continue His blessings on our next generation of fourteen grandchildren. He's promised to shower His *"mercies on thousands of those who love and obey his commandments."*

These blessings are poured out not just on some missionary families, but on all who are faithful to Him in all walks of life. I have Christian friends whom God has blessed for generations in the business world. I know families of farmers God has wonderfully blessed generation after generation. The point is that God blesses families who love Him and heed His commandments. Serious problems come when we let our guard down and permit our concept of the true God to become corrupted. We must never forget what Moses told us:

> *He proclaimed his covenant, which he commanded you to keep—the Ten Commandments— and wrote them on two stone tablets. It was at that time that the LORD commanded me to issue the laws*

and regulations you must obey in the land you are about to enter and occupy. But be careful! You did not see the Lord's form on the day he spoke to you from the fire at Mount Sinai. So do not corrupt yourselves by making a physical image in any form--whether of a man or a woman, an animal or a bird, a creeping creature or a fish. And when you look up into the sky and see the sun, moon, and stars--all the forces of heaven--don't be seduced by them and worship them. The LORD your God designated these heavenly bodies for all the peoples of the earth (Deuteronomy 4:13-19).

Christianized trinkets

Walk into most Christian bookstores today and you'll find plenty of what I call "Christianized trinkets." Not that long ago we'd go to a bookstore to find good books. Not true anymore. In today's bookstores we find everything from coffee and rolls to the latest CD or DVD collections. And trinkets seem to command more and more shelf space. This is especially true in Latin America. Let me say something about it, since I see a potential problem brewing even in North America.

For instance, we've become accustomed to watching our famous athletes either crossing themselves or pulling out a little chain with a cross and kissing it before making a play, believing that act will bring them success. This superstitious search for a blessing or for good luck is what I'm talking about. The idea is spreading that these symbols or trinkets influence what we do.

Such symbols are available in every shape, covering every superstition imaginable: Christianized magnets, key chains, pins, cards, plaques, and even "holy water" from the Jordan and "holy sand" from Israel. Of course, none of these items in and of themselves are bad. Symbols have served the church well for centuries. What's bad is the subtle change that takes place when a symbol becomes an icon—an object that can bring blessing, good fortune, or protection. When someone places faith in an object, a substitute for God has been created. Such an object, then, has in fact become an idol.

God has told us very clearly: *"You must not make for yourself an idol of any kind or an image of anything in the heavens or on the earth or in the sea."*

What a difference it makes when our eyes focus only on the true and living God. He's so much more real and present and powerful and helpful than some trifling object. Instead of trusting in a small, petty, meaningless object, how much more important it is to trust and believe in God Himself. In fact, how can a mere object be compared to the living and all-powerful God?

I'm reminded of a letter we got from a pastor in Ecuador, a pastor we help through our LOGOI ministry. The joy of the discovery of God comes out in every word:

I was an elder in the Mormon Church. I now marvel at how I believed this was the only truth in the whole world. I served as the right hand to the bishop and even baptized various people and visited inactive members with other Mormons. To be a better Mormon I stopped drinking coffee for a year and a half and attended meetings every Sunday. Then God permitted me to come down with an illness. While in the hospital a college friend introduced me to Christ and I came to know the real Omnipotent God, and He became my personal Savior...

Since becoming a Christian, my life has been transformed. I now know and experience the grace and love of God. He gives me a strong internal peace that helps me follow Him, not because I feel obligated, but because I love Him. I love Him because He loved me first. When I was spiritually blind He gave me sight to see the glory of the Christ of the cross.

Carlos Pérez Flores

When we come face to face with the living God, no substitute will do. He meets every need we have, He satisfies every want. We bask in the glory of His love, in the majesty and splendor of His gracious presence. We want no other God.

THE THIRD COMMANDMENT

You must not misuse the name of the LORD your God. The LORD will not let you go unpunished if you misuse his name (Exodus 20:7).

Back in 1674, church leaders gathered at Westminster, in London, made a study of the Ten Commandments. These are the questions and answers they gave to the third commandment:

What is required in the third commandment?
The third commandment requires the holy and reverent use of God's names, titles, attributes, ordinances, Word, and works.

What is forbidden in the third commandment?
The third commandment forbids all profaning or abusing of anything whereby God makes himself known.

What is the reason annexed to
the third commandment?

[In other words, what added reason makes this commandment so important?] The reason annexed to the third commandment is, that however the breakers of this commandment may escape punishment from men, yet the Lord our God will not suffer them to escape his righteous judgment.

A good friend, Stuart Briscoe, told me about a boy who at the dinner table decided to try out a new word he'd learned at school that day. His mother gasped. His father cringed. His brother and sister were horrified. The boy's mother ordered her son to his room, telling him he couldn't come out until that word was totally erased from his vocabulary.

Later that night there was a terrible storm. Lightning turned the night to day and the thunder rolled across the woods making everything tremble. Worried about her son alone in his room, the mother went to check up on him. When she opened the door, she saw him standing by the window shouting: "Lord, all of this just because of that one little word?"

Back when my boys were in their teens, I was able to get them a summer job working at a warehouse owned by a Christian friend. Everything went well for the first few days. The boys seemed happy earning some money, and I was pleased they'd all gotten work at the same place. Plus, I was sure some good old manual labor would be good for them.

Then, one mid-afternoon, my oldest returned home with his two brothers in tow.

"Why are you home so early?" I asked.

"We quit," my oldest son blurted out rather nervously.

"You quit?" I said irritated. "Why in the world would you do that?"

"Dad, we don't like working for your friend. He got mad and cussed everybody out."

"He did what?" I said. "What are you talking about?"

Seeing my frustration, the boys explained, "Dad, your friend got real mad and started cussing everyone, even using God's name. We asked him not to talk like that, but it only made him madder. So we quit."

As I listened, I tried to imagine what my sons had experienced. It wasn't as if they'd never heard someone curse, they heard foul language every day at school. The shocking thing to them was to hear a person whom I'd built up as a strong Christian angrily taking the Lord's name in vain. It was a terrible, disheartening shock which made them (and me) not only lose respect for the man, but even to question his relationship with God.

The great honor that comes with the name
In this commandment we study the honor due the

name of God. We're told that we must not misuse it, nor to take His name in vain. The word "vain," pronounced *shawv* in Hebrew, has two meanings: "perversity" and "vanity." The meaning is clear: it's *perverse* to take God's name and use it in a *vulgar* way. Furthermore, when someone who's not a Christian pretends to be one, he uses the Lord's name in vain. God the Father, God the Son and God the Holy Spirit are so holy and so sacred that everyone on this planet is instructed to protect and honor His name, Christian and non-Christian alike.

We're to continuously praise His name and tell the world about His mighty acts.

Everything about God and His character is wrapped up in His name: His grand titles, His glorious attributes, His clear regulations, His incomparable acts, and everything about His indescribable, glorious being. His name represents everything about Him. It's because of His name that He is *"slow to anger and rich in unfailing love and faithfulness"* (Exodus 34:6-7). It's because of His name that He *"keeps you safe"* (Psalms 20:1). It's because of His name that *"the LORD will not abandon his people"* (1Samuel 12:22). It's because of His name that *"He guides [us] along right paths"* (Psalm 23:3). It's because of His name that our *"sins have been forgiven"* (1John 2:12). It's because of His name that we receive life, strength, joy, and power.

As God's children, we're given access to His glorious

name when we pray, preach, teach, think, or tell others about Him. Also, because of our relationship to Him, His name is to be on our lips when we're sick, in danger, or going through difficult times. Because of His incomparable greatness we're to continuously praise His name and tell the world about His mighty acts.

Not that long ago the *Da Vinci Code* movie became a huge religious controversial news item. The most high and holy Son of God was portrayed as an ordinary man, with the sins and the habits of ordinary people. The misrepresentation of Jesus caused great indignation among Christians. As if that were not enough, soon after came what most Christians thought to be the equally blasphemous *Gospel of Judas* presenting Jesus as unholy and the defender of Judas, one of the most despicable traitors in history.

These acts represent public examples of what this third commandment condemns. God's name must never be used in disrespect. Deuteronomy 28:58 tells us to *"fear the glorious and awesome name of the LORD your God."* John Calvin, in his catechism (the section devoted to the Ten Commandments) adds that this commandment "admonishes us in general, never to utter the name of God unless with fear and reverence, and for the purpose, of honoring it. For while it is thrice holy, we ought to guard, by all means, against seeming to hold it in contempt…" This is done, he says, "by never speaking or thinking of God and his works without honor."

Another way we misuse His name is by assigning to Satan and his demons powers similar to those of God. Consider how degrading and disrespectful this is to God's incomparable name. Furthermore, when we tell jokes that reduce God to a human level, no matter how funny they may seem to us, we disrespect His name. In our service to God, when we attribute to ourselves the honor that alone belongs to Him, we disrespect His name. When we pray in Jesus' name seeking our will instead of His, we disrespect God's name. When we go to church and sing praises to the greatness and glory of God, but then carelessly disobey Him when we leave church, we disrespect God's name. When we use the name of Jesus as a "good-luck" charm, or by thinking the name itself has magical power, we disrespect God's name. When we tell our friends and neighbors about Christ, but live in disobedience to the Gospel, we disrespect God's name.

The commandment tells us: *"You must not misuse the name of the LORD your God."* When we insincerely pray or sing or speak about the Lord, we're breaking the third commandment. When His name is on our lips, but we're not really thinking about what we're saying or how we're using it, we're breaking the third commandment. When we thoughtlessly use such expressions as "Oh, my God!" or "Jesus!" or "My Lord," or "God Almighty," we're breaking the third commandment.

The meaning of the third commandment

I'd like to think that most who misuse His name, particularly in general conversation, do so unintentionally. However, the commandment says: *"The LORD will not let you go unpunished if you misuse his name."* We may not intend to break His commandment or commit this sin, but our lack of intention isn't an acceptable excuse to God. Let me state it as simply as I can: all trivial and thoughtless references to His name are offensive to Him.

Jesus Himself warned us: *"On judgment day many will say to me, 'Lord! Lord! We prophesied in your name and cast out demons in your name and performed many miracles in your name.' But I will reply, 'I never knew you. Get away from me, you who break God's laws.'"* (Matthew 7:22-23). God warns us about "false prophets" whose true aim is to enhance their personal fortunes, rather than bring glory to His name. Jesus clearly exposes them. He doesn't deny that they may do miracles in His name, but declares that He doesn't know them, that they don't belong to Him, that they're far from Him. By what they do they're breaking the Third Commandment.

More and more we hear comments like "God told me…" or "God spoke to me…" followed by some kind of explanation. If the person actually made up the statement, by attributing it to God to gain acceptance or credibility, he or she breaks the third commandment. Similarly, by applying special formulas that use the name of Jesus or Christ in an attempt to heal the sick or to cast out demons, the Lord's name can be misused. This is what Balaam, the false Old Testament prophet did. He used God's name in his incantations or when he performed miracles. He didn't love God; he simply used His name, and wanted to be paid for his favors. God is angered when people use his name hypocritically or for personal gain.

Some two hundred years ago, John Wesley, founder of the Methodist Church, made a comment about this third commandment that, despite its old English style, is worth repeating:

> The third commandment is concerning the manner of our worship…We have a strict prohibition: *"Thou shalt not take the name of the Lord thy God in vain."* We take God's name in vain: **First**, by hypocrisy, making profession of God's name, but not living up to that profession. **Secondly**, by covenant breaking. If we make promises to God, and perform not to the Lord our vows, we take his name in vain. **Thirdly**, by rash swearing, mentioning the name of God, or any of his attributes, in the form of an oath, without any just occasion for it, but to no purpose, or to no good purpose. **Fourthly**, by false-swearing, which some think is chiefly intended in the letter of the commandment. **Fifthly**, by using the name of God lightly

and carelessly. The profanation of the form of devotion is forbidden, as well as the profanation of the forms of swearing; as also, the profanation of any of those things whereby God makes himself known… God will himself be the avenger of those that take his name in vain; and they will find it a fearful thing to fall into the hands of the living God (Hebrews 10:31).

The ease in which God's name is misused

Today it seems virtually impossible to walk the streets, enter a restaurant, or even walk through a park without hearing God's name used offensively. Newspapers, magazines, soap operas, theater, radio and television continually mock or carelessly use the name of God without giving it a thought. This type of disregard for God, the prophet Jeremiah explains, has consequences: *"For the land is full of adultery, and it lies under a curse. The land itself is in mourning—its wilderness pastures are dried up"* (Jeremiah 23:10).

> *God is angered when people use his name hypocritically or for personal gain.*

Because people today so openly abuse the name of God we may have thought that the warning given at the end of this commandment is no longer in effect, that God no longer punishes those who disrespect Him. Let's not forget, however, that the Lord hasn't changed. He's the same today, yesterday and forever. We're told that the *"LORD will not let you go unpunished if you misuse his name."*

During my Bible college years I had a good friend whose first name was John. Both of us planned to become preachers. I envied John because he was so good at speaking, especially telling jokes—a gift relished by preachers. Most of his jokes were good and very funny, but a change occurred during his last year in school. He started telling "religious" jokes. Most of his jokes were original, but all too often they spoke lightly of God or of Jesus. It bothered me so much that I got two of my buddies to go with me and talk to him about it. He shrugged it off. He loved the reaction and laughter he got from his jokes too much to change.

A week or so before our graduation, a local businessman, looking for full-time truck drivers, came to our college. His company delivered all types of merchandise throughout western Canada. As I remember, John was the only one who accepted the job. A week after graduation he started driving a truck.

Imagine our shock to learn that John died in terrible accident on his very first day at work. Several of us got to talking about it, recalling how we had talked to him about his jokes and the warnings we had given him. One classmate asked, "Could the accident have been a direct punishment from God because of the way John so carelessly misused His name?"

Needless to say, John's death left a deep impression

on me. It forced me to ask how God treats us when we disobey His commandments. Is God a vengeful God who zaps us whenever we disobey one of His laws? That's not what I read in Exodus 34:6 and 7, that He is a *"God of compassion and mercy...slow to anger...filled with unfailing love and faithfulness... and lavish[es] unfailing love to a thousand generations."* Neither is it the description of God given in Psalm 85:2: *"You forgave the guilt of your people—yes, you covered all their sins."* Then John 3:16: *"God loved the world so much that he gave his one and only Son, so that everyone who believes in him will not perish but have eternal life."* Jesus took our punishment. He paid for every one of our sins in full.

How, then, does the law of God work? Paul, writing to the Romans, explains the process. First, the law describes the sin—in this particular commandment, the sin is misusing God's holy name. It then points out the one who has disregarded and broken the law. It condemns him and leaves him wallowing in misery over what he has done and said. In that miserable state the sinner cries out: *"What a miserable person I am! Who will free me from this life that is dominated by sin?"* At this point he discovers the main purpose of the law: not to give God occasion to zap him; not to tell a person how to be good; not to hold a person back from sinning; not merely to give instruction as to what God expects of him. The purpose of the law is to convince the sinner he is condemned and desperately needs a Savior. Its purpose is to drive the transgressors to Christ, so that he finds forgiveness and restoration and the power in God to live according to God's standards.

We must take this commandment to heart. Our words matter. Our profession matters. Because we belong to God and have taken His name, we really do need to pray, *"Our Father in heaven, may your name be honored."* And, because we call ourselves Christians (which means "a Christ one"), our challenge is to live and to talk like one.

THE FOURTH COMMANDMENT

Remember to observe the Sabbath day by keeping it holy. You have six days each week for your ordinary work, but the seventh day is a Sabbath day of rest dedicated to the LORD your God. On that day no one in your household may do any work. This includes you, your sons and daughters, your male and female servants, your livestock, and any foreigners living among you. For in six days the LORD made the heavens, the earth, the sea, and everything in them; but on the seventh day he rested. That is why the LORD blessed the Sabbath day and set it apart as holy (Exodus 20:8-11).

What's so all-important about
observing the Lord's Day?

Are there really things we're not supposed
to do on Sunday?

What's Sunday got to do with
our work and leisure?

ERIC LIDDELL, the famous "Flying Scotsman," wonderfully portrayed in the film, *Chariots of Fire*, reminded us how very special the Lord's Day is. His refusal to run on Sunday in the 1924 Olympics wasn't intended as criticism of all the other athletes for not observing the Sabbath, nor was it an act to impress the news media. Liddell's refusal was born out of a sincere belief that the fourth commandment–to remember the Sabbath, to keep it holy– was God's directive to all men. Liddell believed it was wrong to dishonor the Sabbath and was willing to give up fame and fortune to honor God. Not even Prince Philip could make him change his mind.

Interestingly, this is the only commandment that changes between the Old and New Testaments.

On a lighter note, there's the story of a pastor of a Puritan church in New England, before the days of automobiles. One freezing Sunday, rather than walking to church, he decided to skate down the frozen road from his home. When the elders saw him arrive, they immediately gathered in formal session. Had the Sabbath laws been broken? Should the pastor be placed under discipline? After much debate they reached their conclusion: "We'll grant our pastor permission to skate to church on Sundays, but under no circumstance is he to enjoy it."

How are we to observe the Sabbath today? Perhaps

another issue is even more important: if we're to give strict obedience to this commandment, shouldn't we go to church on Saturday rather than Sunday?

Should we worship on Saturday or Sunday?

Interestingly, this is the only commandment that changes between the Old and New Testaments. I rarely hear discussion of this "change" here in the States, but in Latin America the success of Seventh Day Adventists has made this an issue of sufficient significance that we're constantly defending it. At a recent seminar in Colombia a pastor said: "Several people in my church have charged that every Sunday we're breaking the Fourth Commandment, because God tells us to celebrate His day on Saturday. Are they correct?"

I usually explain that the New Testament tells of no debates that took place in the early church on the subject. Rather, we've four brief statements referring to the Lord's Day, telling us that the early Christians made the change. No formal explanation is given:

1. John 20:19: *That **Sunday evening** the disciples were meeting behind locked doors because they were afraid of the Jewish leaders. Suddenly, Jesus was standing there among them! 'Peace be with you,' he said."*

2. Acts 20:7: *"On **the first day of the week**, we gathered to share in the Lord's Supper. Paul was preaching to them, and since he was leaving the next day…"*

3.   1Corinthians 16:2: *"On **the first day of each week**, you should each put aside a portion of the money you have earned..."*

4.   Revelation 1:9-10: *"I, John, am your brother and your partner in suffering... It was the **Lord's Day**, and I was worshiping in the Spirit..."*

There's no indication whatsoever that the early church was in turmoil because the change was made to observe the Lord's Day on Sunday. It's possible that some Jewish Christians did object and for this reason Paul, in his letter to the Colossians, states: *"...don't let anyone condemn you for what you eat or drink, or for not celebrating certain holy days or new-moon ceremonies or Sabbaths"* (Colossians 2:16). Surely, if the Sunday observance was dishonoring God, Paul would have said so on this, or other occasions. Instead he told the Gentile believers not to pay attention to the condemnations being made concerning their days of worship. Nowhere in the New Testament does it say that the Jewish *Shabbat* should be observed.

Acts 15 details the first great Church Council in Jerusalem. They agree to write the spiritual require-ments the Gentile, non-Jewish believers, are to follow as related to the Law:

> *This letter is from the apostles and elders, your brothers in Jerusalem...For it seemed good to the Holy Spirit and to us to lay no greater burden on you than these requirements: You must abstain from eating food offered to idols, from*

> consuming blood or eating the meat of strangled
> animals, and from sexual immorality. If you do
> this, you will do well... (Acts 15:23-29).

Nothing at all is said about the *Sabbath*. One simply has to remember how important the Sabbath was to the Jews to understand that this omission is especially significant. In other words, had the celebration of a specific day been important for Gentile believers, surely it would have been mentioned here.

Aside from these biblical observations some historic evidences can also be added. The resurrection of Jesus, three days after His crucifixion, far surpassed all the amazing miracles the early Christians had ever witnessed. It was more impressive than all the miracles they'd read about in their Old Testament manuscripts. Jesus' amazing miraculous resurrection once and for all established the absolute

There's no indication that the early church was in turmoil because the change was made to observe the Lord's Day on Sunday.

truthfulness of all He'd said and done. That man they had known, watched, talked to, walked with, touched, listened to, and had seen die at the hands of Roman soldiers on Calvary, and buried in a tomb sealed by a boulder, had come back to life–just as He said He would! They'd seen Him! They'd talked to Him! They'd touched his scarred hands! They'd looked at the spear-wound in his side! He was indisputably as alive as alive could be! Death had lost its hold on Him! Nothing they had heard or seen or dreamed about could possibly match the glory of that fact. And its significance left its indelible impression. He actually did come back from the dead. The promise he'd made that they too would live again was now just as real as the miracle they'd witnessed!

Here was reason indeed to celebrate. The *Sabbath*– with all its prohibitions, all its details, all its demands– had been wearisome, if not fearsome. Sunday–with all its splendor, glory, power, and promise–was by contrast as different as life is from death. To celebrate Sunday meant the celebration of life itself. Automatically, then, without being told or instructed, they gathered on this memorable day to remember everything Jesus meant to them.

Did Adam and Eve and the earth's early descendants observe the Sabbath?

A custom was born that's lasted to this day. There's been no need to defend it, its significance speaks for itself. Its replacement of the *Shabbat* has brought special life and meaning to Christianity and great glory to the Eternal Father of our resurrected Lord and Savior. After 2000 years of celebration, no church council and no debate or argument has persuaded the Christian church to return to the old patterns and observance of Saturday.

When did Sabbath worship begin?

The study of Sabbath worship rightly begins in the comments we find in Genesis:

> *On the seventh day God had finished his work of creation, so he rested from all his work. And God blessed the seventh day and declared it holy, because it was the day when he rested from all his work of creation* (Genesis 2: 2-3).

This early mention of "God's day of rest" has created what is called the "historical problem." Did Adam and Eve and the earth's early descendants observe the Sabbath? When, actually, was the first Sabbath observed? Did its observance begin after Moses received the Ten Commandments? If so, was the Sabbath observance something for everyone, or was this a law just for the Israelites?

Those who argue the Sabbath was meant only for the Israelites cite Nehemiah 9:13-14 to make their point:

> *You came down at Mount Sinai and spoke to them from heaven. You gave them regulations and instructions that were just, and decrees and commands that were good. You instructed them concerning your holy Sabbath. And you commanded them, through Moses your servant, to obey all your commands, decrees, and instructions.*

According to those verses, it would seem that Moses was the first to receive the commandment.

Secondly, reading about the entire period covered

by the book of Genesis, the Sabbath isn't mentioned once. Although Abraham, Isaac and Jacob received instructions about sacrifices (Genesis 4:3-4), altars (Genesis 8:20), priests (Genesis 14:18), offerings (Genesis 14:20), circumcision (Genesis 17:10), and marriage (Genesis 2:24 and 34:9), nothing at all is said about the Sabbath. We can conclude that since the commandment is not mentioned from Adam to Moses, the first centuries of believers didn't observe it. The question then arises, why were Abraham and the other patriarchs not instructed to observe the Sabbath?

A third observation can be drawn from Deuteronomy 5:15. We read that Moses was given this commandment for a special reason:

> Remember that you were once slaves in Egypt,
> but the LORD your God brought you out with
> his strong hand and powerful arm. That is why
> the LORD your God has commanded you to rest
> on the Sabbath day.

This verse seems to indicate that the observance of the Lord's Day wasn't solely based on God's resting on the seventh day as related in Genesis 2:2-3. Instead, the Israelites were given this Sabbath day to remind them how God powerfully freed them from slavery in Egypt.

In addition, Exodus 31:17 clearly states that the observance of the Sabbath isn't something God imposed on the world, but instead is a special covenant (or agreement) between God and the people of Israel, again making reference to the original meaning in Genesis 2.

> It is a permanent sign of my covenant with the people of Israel. For in six days the LORD made heaven and earth, but on the seventh day he stopped working and was refreshed.

Jesus Himself brings all these arguments to a fitting conclusion when He explains:

> Don't misunderstand why I have come. I did not come to abolish the Law of Moses or the writings of the prophets. No, I came to accomplish their purpose. I tell you the truth, until heaven and earth disappear, not even the smallest detail of God's law will disappear until its purpose is achieved. So if you ignore the least commandment and teach others to do the same, you will be called the least in the Kingdom of Heaven. But anyone who obeys God's laws and teaches them will be called great in the Kingdom of Heaven. (Matthew 5:17-19).

How are we to observe the Sabbath?

Our obligation as Christians, first, is to recognize that the fourth commandment does apply to us. But, on this so called "day of rest," are we to do nothing other than go to church, pray and read the Bible? Can we also practice or even play a sport, cook meals, and enjoy the day with the family? How are we to observe this commandment?

There's no doubt that if we observe the fourth commandment as it was observed in Old Testament days, the celebration becomes controversial. For instance, in Exodus 35 we're told that no household activity was allowed on the Sabbath. It was forbidden to even light a fire for cooking. Should we apply the same rigor in our observance as the ancient Jews? Should we take the same approach as the English Puritans? An example of their Sabbath beliefs is found in the 1648 Westminster Shorter Catechism:

How did Jesus observe the Sabbath?

> *The Sabbath is to be sanctified by a holy resting all that day, even from such worldly employments and recreations as are lawful on other days; and spending the whole time in the public and private exercises of God's worship, except so much as is to be taken up in the works of necessity and mercy.(Luke 4:16; 20:7)... The reasons annexed to the fourth commandment are, God's allowing us six days of the week for our own employments, his challenging a special propriety in the seventh, his own example, and his blessing the Sabbath day.*

A better question would be, how did Jesus observe the Sabbath? His observance of the day must certainly be the right one. But, first, let's take a closer look at a few other details involved in this fourth commandment.

Six days a week are set apart for our daily duties

This stipulation deals with a universal principle: man needs to work. Some people mistakenly believe that work is God's punishment for Adam and Eve's sin in the Garden. But before the fall we read: *"The LORD God placed the man in the Garden of Eden to tend and watch over it"* (Genesis 2:15). Obviously, our first parents were given a huge job. The work we do has always been an important aspect of our humanity. Through our work we show who we are and our unique abilities. Our achievements demonstrate we're creatures who have a likeness to God because of the great variety of things we can do.

Jesus himself said: *"My Father is always working, and so am I"* (John 5:17). The very first chapter of the Bible describes God at work. His accomplishments were unsurpassable: *"Then God looked over all he had made, and he saw that it was very good"* (Genesis 1:31). Our work as humans also defines us as special creatures made by a working and creative God. This is evident whether we're carpenters, homemakers, plumbers, farmers, teachers, architects, doctors, philosophers, theologians, or whatever our vocation. We demonstrate uniqueness from the rest of creation by the work we do; proof that indeed we're made in the image of God.

Another thing, because of the importance of a good work ethic, the Bible condemns laziness.[1] In 2Thessalonians Paul chastises believers who quit

---

[1] See Ecclesiastes 10:15, 18 and Proverbs 6:6-11; 10:4-5; 12:27; 13:4; 15:19; 18:9; 19:15, 24; 20:4, 13; 22:13; 24:30-34; 26:13-16.

working and began living at the expense of others. He simply declared: *"Those unwilling to work will not get to eat"* (2Thessalonians 3:10).

I remember a summer I worked in a steel mill in Johnstown, Pennsylvania, during my college days. I'd hoped for a nice clean job in an air-conditioned office. That fantasy quickly evaporated the day I reported for work. I was sent with a group of ten or twelve men to a field near the factory where copper scraps had been dumped. The foreman explained how the scraps were to be separated and told us to get to work, then he walked back to his air conditioned office in the mill. I hadn't come dressed for that kind of dirty work, but that didn't matter. I had no choice but to dig in and get dirty.

Since this was my first time to meet these men, I went over and introduced myself. After a few pleasantries, I walked over to the piles of copper and began doing what we'd been told to do. Off to the side someone yelled, "Hey, Thompson. Wha'cha doin'? Take it easy, man. Come over here and let's talk this thing over."

It didn't take long to learn the men had no intention of doing any more work than was absolutely necessary. One of the guys–he'd assumed leadership of the group–spelled out exactly what each of us was expected to do, according to his idea of work. When I objected, he laughed at me and said, "Fine, you go right ahead. The more you do, the less we'll have to do." He sat down next to a pile of metal and lit a cigarette. The others followed suit, all watching me as I began separating the copper into piles according to the instructions we'd received.

A couple of hours later, one of the men shouted that the foreman was on his way back. Immediately, everyone got up and began to work. The foreman walked up and looked us over. "What's your name?" he said, pointing to me.

"Thompson," I said.

Turning to the others, he asked, "How come Thompson's dirty and sweaty and the rest of you aren't?"

Because of the importance of a good work ethic, the Bible condemns laziness.

Nobody said a word.

"Thompson," he said, "come with me." Turning to the others, he said, "Get to work. I'd better see some dirt and sweat next time I come out."

I followed him back to his office. He pointed to an empty desk by a window and said, "Sit there. I was hoping to find someone to serve as my assistant. I think you'll do." The office wasn't very large, but it was air conditioned.

Obviously, a good work ethic has its rewards. It sets people apart. Those who understand the importance of work will give their best efforts with pride. Paul reminds Christians about the attitude they should have: *"And whatever you do or say, do it as a representative of the Lord Jesus, giving thanks through him to God the Father"* (Colossians 3:17). The Christian work ethic begins with the assumption that we're God's representatives. Whatever the work assignment may be, what we do and how we do it reflects on God. We do our very best because that's what God expects of us. Whether washing floors, designing skyscrapers, hammering nails, changing diapers, or preparing a Bible lesson, excellence is the only standard we can legitimately accept. The excuse that we're fallible human beings, that we make mistakes, that everything we do is tainted by sin doesn't fit when it comes to our work ethic. Our natural human abilities and God-given gifts are what count when it comes to our work. To do our best doesn't take talent, it doesn't take brains, it doesn't even take spirituality, it just takes will-power.

The fourth commandment states that God has given us six days to devote to our work. God could have said: "You'll worship me six days and work only one." Instead He gave us six days to fulfill our obligations, commitments and plans, and asked for only one day to specifically rest and honor Him.

Voltaire, during the French Revolution, declared: "If you want to kill Christianity, you must abolish Sunday." The Revolutionary Convention in 1793 tried to do just that. They replaced the Gregorian calendar with a more scientific and rational system that sought to avoid all Christian associations (similar to what

Fidel Castro did when he annulled all Christian celebrations, including Sundays, in Cuba). To honor the ten year anniversary of the foundation of the French Republic in 1792, the Convention designed a "week" of 10 working days. It failed. Workers couldn't handle that many days without rest and became less productive. A solution was suggested by a social scientist: "Reinstate the seven-day week making Sunday a day of rest." Production again increased and the nation returned to normalcy.

Having made us in His image, God knew what we needed: *"You have six days each week for your ordinary work, but the seventh day is a Sabbath day of rest dedicated to the LORD your God."*

A day of rest dedicated to the Lord

The phrase *"the seventh day is a Sabbath day of rest dedicated to the LORD your God"* carries two concepts. The first is a *"day of rest"*—tranquility and quiet, not simply a 30-minute nap. It entails an entire day of rest.

The second concept is a day *"dedicated to the Lord."* It means we've been given an entire day to worship and focus on our Creator the way He deserves.

Time is no doubt the most precious gift God has given us. It includes time to sleep, time to work, time to worship, time for your spouse, time for your children, time for friends, time for legitimate pleasures, time for all kinds of things, as spelled out in Ecclesiastes. To each of us—presidents and plumbers alike—has been given 24 hours in each day. No one can complain that he or she has fewer hours than someone else. Time's been meted out equally. What matters, then, is how we use those God-given hours.

Time is the most precious gift from God.

———∿∿∿∿∿∿∿———

God intended the seventh day to change our routine, as a way to regroup our physical and mental strength and to reinforce our relationship with Him: *"The seventh day is a Sabbath day of rest dedicated to the LORD your God."*

Physical rest and spiritual adoration aren't in conflict with each other, neither are they a contradiction. We can worship and rest at the same time.

David talks of this kind of combination in Psalm 27:4: *The one thing I ask of the LORD--the thing I seek most--is to live in the house of the LORD all the days of my life, delighting in the LORD's perfections and meditating in his Temple.*

He repeats the idea in Psalm 23:6: *"Surely your goodness and unfailing love will pursue me all the days of my life, and I will live in the house of the LORD forever."* Granted, this verse is normally interpreted as having to do with our eternal rest. However, David could've been thinking just as easily of the present, life-long delight of experiencing and enjoying God every single day.

As a busy king, David couldn't have meant he desired to abandon his throne and responsibilities to spend all day in the temple worshiping God. His words must've had a different meaning. For David — as well as for you and me— *"the house of the Lord"* meant the place where God was present, not necessarily the physical temple. The office, the farm, the store, the factory, the home all become God's temple when we practice the reality of the presence of God. Saint Paul agrees. In 2Corinthians 6:16 he says: *"For we are the temple of the living God. As God said: 'I will live in them and walk among them…'"*

God isn't found only in buildings we call "churches" or "temples." He's not locked in by four walls, anxiously awaiting our visit on Sundays. When he dedicated the most magnificent temple ever built, Solomon said: *"Why, even the highest heavens cannot contain you. How much less this Temple I have built!"* (1Kings 8:27). God is wherever we are. He's everywhere. We enjoy Him by recognizing that the *house of the Lord* is everywhere we happen to be. We enjoy Him by recognizing that wherever we are, even in the most adverse of circumstances, we are *"in the house of the LORD."* While this recognition is for every single day of the week, God's given us one special day each week when we're to stop all our obligations and in a myriad ways contemplate His incomparable majesty and splendor.

No one may do any kind of work…
The Jewish Sabbath was a day of absolute rest:

On that day no one in your household may do any work. This includes you, your sons and daughters, your male and female servants, your livestock, and any foreigners living among you.

I searched on the internet for ways the Jews observe the Sabbath today. Here's one answer I found: "In the Jewish community, regardless of whether one is orthodox or conservative, keeping the Sabbath is an important sign that indicates one is a Jew. It's the sign God gave Israel from Mount Sinai to distinguish his people from the rest of the world. When you travel to Israel on a Saturday, all stores are closed, public transportation is discontinued and there's no activity in Old Jerusalem for 24 hours."

Orthodox Jews may neither start nor put out a fire on Saturday, therefore they use what's come to be called the 'Sabbath Gentile'–usually someone in need of a hand-out, whom they pay a few cents to light a stove, or turn on a light switch so that they don't have to 'work.' These pious Jews are certainly bound by the letter of God's Law rather than by its spirit.

James Burton Coffman,[2] former minister of the Manhattan Church of Christ in New York City, notes that in the course of 50 years the Jews were commanded to keep eight different classes of Sabbath days. Leviticus 26:2 says: *"You must keep my Sabbath days…"* (note the use of plural).

---

[2] *The Ten Commandments Yesterday and Today*, Fleming H. Revell, New Yersey, p. 50.

The Sabbath Day (Saturday)	2,600 days
Passover	100 days
Day of First Fruits	50 days
Feast of Trumpets	50 days
Sabbaths of Years	2,520 days
Year of Jubilee	365 days
Days of Atonement	50 days
Total in 50 years:	5,785 days

Coffman adds: "The Sabbaths add up to nearly sixteen years, or more than a fourth of the 50-year period. That the Jews themselves didn't keep these Sabbaths in any satisfactory manner is obvious. No wonder Paul referred to the whole system as a "...*slavery to the law*" (Galatians 5:1), and Peter agreed when he said it was a "...*yoke that neither we nor our ancestors were able to bear*" (Acts 15:10).

Imagine what the Pharisees thought of Jesus when they saw Him arbitrarily break their Sabbath laws. The New Testament tells us He did all the following on the Sabbath:

- He healed a man who was born blind (John 9:13-38).
- He healed the paralyzed man from Bethesda (John 5:1-18).
- He healed a man who suffered from dropsy (Luke 14:1).
- Jesus saw a man with a deformed hand and healed him (Mark 3:1-6).
- He saw and healed a woman who was bent

over and couldn't stand up straight (Luke 13:10-12).

A proper question for us would be to ask how Jesus kept the Sabbath, and then for us to keep the Sabbath in the same spirit. As we study the Gospels we discover the following:

1. Luke 4:16 says *"When he came to the village of Nazareth, his boyhood home, he went as usual to the synagogue on the Sabbath and stood up to read the Scriptures."* He faithfully went to the synagogue on Saturdays. Like him, we should go to church. The Bible tells us of others who followed the same tradition. Paul and Barnabas observed the Sabbath as well. Acts 13:14 says: *"On the Sabbath they went to the synagogue for the services."*

    Conclusion: We should be faithful church attendees on Sundays.

2. Jesus showed the people of Israel they'd misinterpreted the commandment, and publicly broke the Sabbath rules imposed by the Pharisees.

    Conclusion: It's easy for us to create man-made rules or to exaggerate Bible requirements. We're to obey the rules given us by God, not those invented by men.

3. Jesus explained that his Father wanted people *"to show mercy, not offer sacrifices"* (Mathew 12:7). He asked in Mark 3: *"Does the law permit good deeds on the Sabbath, or is it a day for doing evil? Is this a day to save life or to destroy it?"*

Conclusion: Sunday's a day we should use to help the needy. We can do so through our tithes and offerings, by visiting the sick and disadvantaged, and by helping the needy in countless ways.

4. Jesus added that Saturday was made to help and bless mankind, not to find an excuse to condemn them (Mark 2:23-28).

   Conclusion: Don't emphasize the weaknesses in people. Instead, find ways to encourage people to remain strong and to trust God no matter their circumstances and problems.

5. Jesus concluded with a stern declaration: He, not Moses, was Lord, *even of the Sabbath.* He was to determine what was allowed and what was forbidden (Luke 6:1-5).

   Conclusion: That which has been created, like the Sabbath, isn't to be considered greater or more important than the Creator. Nothing is more important than God. We worship Him, not a day.

Popular talk-show host and author, Dr. Laura Schlesinger,[3] offers the following suggestions on how to observe the Sabbath properly. I believe God would approve of her advice:

- Don't work for pay and don't compete for awards on the Sabbath.
- Take time to relax and do nothing. (Even if it's not specified in the Bible, a nap during

---

[3] *The Ten Commandments*, Dr. Laura Schlessinger, HarperCollins, New York, 2006, p.112.

the Sabbath is truly a divine gift.)

- Read and study good religious books.
- Play with your children and spouse; enjoy your family.
- Take a walk.
- Enjoy a delicious meal and spend time with friends.
- Talk to your children about their daily life, their thoughts and feelings.
- Attend religious services, conferences and talks.
- Pray and meditate.

Personally, I believe what matters is that we embrace the true spirit of rest and worship God has requested of us—breaking from the daily routine and weekly obligations and finding special ways to worship God. Also, remember that to show the Pharisees were wrong to maintain their strict customs, Jesus spent many Sabbaths helping others. Should we not also remember to follow Jesus' example on our day of rest by helping people in need?

God created the Sabbath to help us break our weekly routine so that we might leave the stress of our jobs, and also to free us from the materialism that so easily controls our lives. Jesus, through the Sabbath, reminds us that *"People do not live by bread alone, but by every word that comes from the mouth of God"* (Matthew 4:4).

THE FIFTH COMMANDMENT

Honor your father and mother. Then you will live a long, full life in the land the LORD your God is giving you (Exodus 20:12).

**What's so important about our relationship
to our fathers and mothers
that God would write
a special commandment about it?**

T HE FIFTH COMMANDMENT serves as a great bridge. The first four deal with our relationship to God, the remaining six with our relationships to others. As we look, study and absorb each of the ten, we begin to see why Jesus could summarize them into two:

> *You must love the LORD your God with all your heart, all your soul, and all your mind. This is*

the first and greatest commandment. A second is equally important: Love your neighbor as your-self. The entire law and all the demands of the prophets are based on these two commandments. (Matthew 22:37-40).

Precisely, the first four commandments tell us how to love God; and the last six tell us how to love our neighbors. For instance, commandments five, six and seven help us get rid of self absorbing love; while the last three show us how to keep peace and love flowing with our neighbors.

Neighborly love, we quickly discover as we look at the first one of these final commandments, begins by showing honor and respect for our parents; assuming, of course, that children know their parents and are able to honor them as they deserve.

The Grimm brothers, back in 1812, could have been thinking about this commandment when they wrote their fable, *The Old Grandfather and His Grandson:*

Once upon a time there was a very, very old man. His eyes had grown dim, his ears deaf, and his knees shook. When he sat at the table, he could scarcely hold a spoon. He spilled soup on the tablecloth, and, besides that, some of his soup would run back out of his mouth.

His son and his son's wife were disgusted with this, so finally they made the old grandfather sit in the corner behind the stove, where they gave him his food in an earthenware bowl, and not enough at that. He sat there looking sadly at the table, and his eyes grew moist. One day his shaking hands could not hold the bowl, and it fell to the ground and broke. The young woman scolded him, but he said not a word. He only sobbed. Then for a few pennies they bought him a wooden bowl and made him eat from it.

Neighborly love begins by showing honor and respect for our parents.

Once when they were all sitting there, the little grandson of four years pushed some pieces of wood together on the floor.

"What are you making?" asked his father.

"Oh, I'm making a little trough for you and mother to eat from when you're old."

The man and the woman looked at one another and then began to cry. They immediately brought the old grandfather to the table, and always let him eat there from then on. And if he spilled a little, they didn't say a thing.

Sometimes, in the endless hustle and bustle of our modern world it's easy to forget the truly important things. In simple and direct words, God gives us a very important responsibility: *"Honor your father and your mother."*

How we honor our parents

The Hebrew word, *kavod* (honor), originates from

kavad, which means "something heavy." The responsibility to honor our parents isn't always easy—especially when they reach a certain age. The burden can become very heavy.

When my wife Carolyn's mother died, she and I took over the care of her father. My father-in-law had been a faithful and loving pastor, and had always treated me like a son. We gladly readjusted our lives to bring him into our home, ignoring the costs and sacrifices involved.

As time went by, and his needs became greater, caring for him became more and more difficult. Eventually we had to find a nurse to help take care of him. Then his memory began to fade. It was especially hard on my wife when the father she loved no longer recognized her. The task grew heavier as the months turned into years. And then he had a stroke and we had to take him to the hospital. A few days later, with a smile full of joy, and his hand pointing to heaven, he entered into the presence of the Lord.

Now, as I look back on that experience, I realize the many sacrifices that were involved in taking care of an elderly parent. We had to prepare a room and equip it especially for him. We had to nurse him and take him to the doctor and provide for all his medications. We had to dress him, bathe him, even make sure he ate. We had to spend many hours keeping him company. We literally had to share our lives with him, sacrificing our own interests in our desire to make him happy.

Caring for him was like that well-known phrase we all repeat at our wedding: "Will you love and honor him in sickness and in health, in good times and bad?" Because we loved him, we accepted the responsibility as a privilege and honor.

At the same time, though difficult, the experience had its rewards. I've never known a kinder person than my father-in-law. His love for Christ permeated everything he did. He always had a smile on his face, a word of encouragement, a firm and loving hand-shake, and a perfect Bible verse for every occasion. It was a joy to hear him pray. There was no doubt that he knew and loved Jesus truly and intimately. As I look back on those years I realize there were many difficult and trying days, nevertheless it was a privilege caring for him. This was the man who had given so much comfort, love, nourishment, and spiritual help to the woman who is my wife and whom I love with all my heart.

The responsibility to honor our parents isn't always easy.

Furthermore, *"Honor your father and mother"* is God's command. And He promises: *"Then you will live a long, full life in the land the LORD your God is giving you."*

The commandment's significance in the Bible

The word "honor" means to show respect and esteem; to confer distinction; to revere. In Old Testament days this commandment was so important that a son who disrespected his father could to be put to death (Exodus 21:17; Leviticus 20:9). We read that God cursed Ham because he was disrespectful to his father Noah (Genesis 9:21-27). In New Testament times Jesus condemned the Pharisees for changing the meaning of the fifth commandment. They permitted children to stop providing for their parents so long as they gave that money to the temple instead (Matthew 15:3-9).

Why is this commandment so important?

1. The family is the foundation of society; when the family structure breaks down, the entire nation begins to crumble. In the book of Malachi, chapter two, God tells Israel He rejects their offerings and no longer accepts their worship. Among the sins mentioned is the breakup of the families and their terrible unfaithfulness to their marriage vows. When God removes His blessings, a nation no longer has stability.

2. The family represents the basic unit from which desperately needed spiritual leaders emerge. In Malachi 2:15, God explains that, because of all the moral infidelity in Israel, the families failed to produce *"godly children."* Fathers and mothers committed to biblical values are the ones who produce children who become strong spiritual leaders. Take King Uzziah as an example: *"He was sixteen years old when he became king, and he reigned in Jerusalem fifty-two years. His mother was Jecoliah from Jerusalem. He did what was pleasing*

in the Lord's sight, just as his father, Amaziah, had done" (2Kings 15:2-3). Note that the mother and the father of the king are both mentioned. It was their godly upbringing that produced their good and godly son, Uzziah. That's what God looks for in all Christian families.

3. It goes without saying that all children owe their parents immense gratitude for the many years parents provided food, clothing, a home and education. How much more, when parents surround that home with

    The family is the foundation of society.

    love and teach their children how to live godly lives in this ungodly world of ours.

4. Children need the protection of parents much more than they realize. This becomes especially obvious when parents become so absorbed in their personal pursuits and ambitions they pay little attention to their children. Rather than a godly example, children see self-centered, selfish parents. Rather than a loving and kind God who is reflected by their parents, children grow up forgotten, uncared for, often abused, to fend for themselves in a hostile and unfriendly environment. Unfortunately, such children, because they know nothing else, usually grow up to reproduce that same type of environment in the homes they establish.

5. Parents, in their old age, generally depend on their children to be their caretakers. Who, however, wants to take care of cantankerous, demanding, unloving old people? If we as parents don't want to end up that way, while we're young and able we should learn to be kind, loving, truthful, generous, and forgiving. Paul has some good advice for us all as families: *"Wives, submit to your husbands, as is fitting for those who belong to the Lord. Husbands, love your wives and never treat them harshly. Children, always obey your parents, for this pleases the Lord. Fathers, do not aggravate your children, or they will become discouraged"* (Colossians 3:18-21).

The quality of life in a society is wonderfully reinforced when this Fifth Commandment is obeyed. Parents whose children love them and care for them live longer, so all of society benefits. When children enjoy the quality of life provided by loving parents, they live with fewer worries and less stress, and this contributes toward longer lives. That precisely is God's promise: *"You will live a long, full life in the land the LORD your God is giving you."*

Additional implications for parents

Parents who want to be honored must themselves be honorable. Abusive or tyrannical parents don't deserve the respect and love of their children. Children, with rare exceptions, love their parents, regardless of how abusive they might have been. The only explanation is that God made us that way; a child instinctively loves his father and mother. However, if that love and trust a child places in his parents is betrayed again and again, there may come a point when that child turns against his parents.

Because this parent-child relationship is so crucial, God warns: *"Fathers, do not provoke your children to anger by the way you treat them"* (Ephesians 6:4). Since God Himself is a father, He's concerned about the way parents behave toward their children. We must never forget that the family has a divine origin. God invented it. He's the one—and not society— who establishes the patterns we're to follow. God clearly tells us that

The quality of life in a society is reinforced when the fifth commandment is obeyed.

the father is to be the leader in the family, because families with good fathers are normally healthy families.

Unfortunately, fatherhood, in the above sense, isn't stressed in some parts of the world. In Latin America, for instance, the mother is the one who's idealized. Custom has established that the father is the one to be feared, not loved; obeyed, but not followed. In his essay *The Labyrinth of Solitude* (1950), Mexican writer, Octavio Paz, explains the historic and cultural catalysts behind these traits. According to Paz:

> The *macho* represents the masculine pole of life. The phrase "I am your father" has

absolutely no paternal flavor. It is not said in order to protect or to guide the child, rather to impose the father's authority, and actually used to humiliate the child... One word sums up the aggressiveness, insensitivity, invulnerability and all the other attributes of the male macho figure: power.

Norma Fuller, Ph.D. (1998) of the Catholic University of Peru, tells us that "[Octavio] Paz has had a profound and lasting impact on all analysts who have tried to understand the problems of the masculine identity in this continent." And further, following the same line of thought, sociologist Sonia Montecino (1992) explains: "The absence of the father figure empowers the maternal figure. This belittles the paternal figure in the child's imagination. As he grows, [the Latin] child identifies home with a negative or absent father figure and a powerful maternal one. This reinforces the myth of the super mother and the irresponsible father."

One of the areas that must be emphasized by preachers in the Latin world is the role of fathers as presented in the Bible. They must be made aware of their historic social tendencies, and then learn the biblical role God has established. Of course, the mother, school, church and society all play significant roles in the life of a child, however, we must emphasize the all-important impact a godly father has on his children.

Parental ideals

It's significant to point out that the fifth commandment separates the role of the father from that of the mother. The commandment doesn't say "honor your parents." It separates these roles. First it says, *"honor your father,"* followed by the second command, *"honor your mother."*

> *As the head of his household a father represents God.*

The moral collapse of the family is rooted in the failure of proper or correct parental ideals. Generally a father is expected to work to provide food, clothing, housing and education for the family. Often he's also considered the "morality policeman" of his children. But, does he realize that as head of his household he represents God? In God's family design the following duties rest squarely on a father's shoulders (the role of the mother is one of loving reinforcement):

- Children will know God by the way their father loves God.
- Children will know right from wrong by their father's actions.
- Children will learn obedience by the way their father obeys God.
- Children will learn respect by the way their father treats others.
- Children will learn the purity of love by the sincerity of their father's love.
- Children will learn to respect women by the

way their father treats and respects their mother.

- Children will learn to tell the truth when their father is a truthful man.
- Children will learn to love God when they see how their father loves Him.
- Children will become good men and women based on their father's example.
- Children will become faithful Christians by following their father's example.

In Hebrew, the word for parents, *horim*, is related to the word *moreh*, or "teacher." God has given parents the responsibility to teach their children. Many fathers try to escape it by saying this is the responsibility of the mother, school or church. But Scripture makes it clear it's the responsibility of both parents. This being the case, since the father is the leader of the household, he needs to take the lead:

- *"And you must commit yourselves wholeheartedly to these commands that I am giving you today. Repeat them again and again to your children. Talk about them when you are at home and when you are on the road, when you are going to bed and when you are getting up. Tie them to your hands and wear them on your forehead as reminders"* (Deuteronomy 6:6-8).
- *"Each generation tells of your faithfulness to the next"* (Isaiah 38:19).
- *"Those who spare the rod of discipline hate their children. Those who love their children care enough*

to discipline them" (Proverbs 13:24).

- *"A youngster's heart is filled with foolishness, but physical discipline will drive it away"* (Proverbs 22:15).

- *"Fathers, do not provoke your children to anger by the way you treat them. Rather, bring them up with the discipline and instruction that comes from the Lord"* (Ephesians 6:4).

- *"Then he put a little child among them. Taking the child in his arms, he said to them, 'Anyone who welcomes a little child like this on my behalf welcomes me, and anyone who welcomes me welcomes not only me but also my Father who sent me'"* (Mark 9:36-37).

- *"Then Jesus called for the children and said to the disciples, "Let the children come to me. Don't stop them! For the Kingdom of God belongs to those who are like these children"'* (Luke 18:16).

I'm eternally grateful to God for giving me a father who recognized his responsibility and taught me not only God's Word but how to be a man, a gentleman and how to follow Christ. By the way he loved my mother I learned how I should love and treat my wife. He was my faithful teacher and guide, first by his example and then by his excellent teachings.

Although we've emphasized the role of the father, we must remember that the emphasis of the fifth commandment actually falls on children. They must honor, respect, obey and love their parents.

Children are to honor their parents

Children normally ask, "Why should I honor Mom and Dad? They demand too much of me. They make too many rules. They never let us do what we want. They're more like dictators than parents. If they really loved us, they'd give us more freedom." For more than 4,000 years the Bible has been giving children the answers. Here's a summary:

1. **We must honor our parents so we can live a "*long life,*" says Exodus 20:12.**

    What has honoring parents got to do with living a long life? Perhaps children don't tie these concepts together because their parents provide everything for them. Most are sheltered, for example, from financial struggles and hardships. It's when they grow up and have to struggle for their own survival that they begin to appreciate what their parents did for them.

2. **We must honor our parents so we can live a "*full life,*" says Deuteronomy 5:16.**

    When children accept their parents' godly authority, the result is the family's emotional stability. Conflict and opposition are replaced by peace. Under such circumstances parents teach their children, explain how the world functions, advise them on the dangers that threaten them, and create a protective shield around their home. Children who are lovingly taught and nourished learn to appreciate their parents' wisdom. The result is a fuller, more rewarding life.

3. **We must honor our parents because it's "the right thing to do," explains Ephesians 6:1.**

When we speak of that which is "right" we refer to what's correct and reasonable. The younger a child, the weaker his understanding of what is right. Consequently, he becomes rebellious in the face of discipline and parental demands. He's too young to understand reasoning. Likewise, teenagers often don't understand their parents' restrictions.

I read the story of a young man who demanded his affluent father buy him a car for his 18th birthday. The father refused because he knew his son was a reckless driver. The son persisted until the father finally gave in. The very first day in his new car, the son tried to see how fast the car would go. He lost control, crashed into a tree and died. Although children may not understand or believe it, most parents set fair and reasonable rules because they love their children and want to protect them. Obedience, then, is the right response for children, even though they might not fully understand all the reasons.

When children accept their parents' godly authority, the result is the family's emotional stability.

4. **We must honor our parents because it**

"pleases the Lord," says Colossians 3:20.

We must recognize the family as one of God's greatest creations. It started in the Garden of Eden and has survived the ages. Few things in this world are as special as a healthy family where husband and wife love each other, parents love their children, and children honor their parents. The divine purpose is accomplished as the family experiences God's blessings and grace. There is love, peace, joy, happiness, and unity, and God is pleased.

God's divine plan is that children honor their parents and that parents are honorable. Only when both parties follow God's instructions do we see the type of families that enjoy God's blessings.

Seek to live by God's commandment

Families who lack the essential values discussed in this chapter are families that live on the border of chaos. It's when God's rules are disregarded that fathers become negligent and abusive and mothers live trapped in their struggles and sorrows. In such cases children live their lives not knowing what "normal" means. They grow up with distorted concepts of life, love, and the world. When they start their own families, they tend to repeat their parents' mistakes, because it's how they were taught. They live their dysfunctional lives believing they're normal. What a contrast to healthy families who love God and are obedient to His laws. Sadly, children are most affected by the lack of biblical principles lived out by their parents.

I've been impressed by the way the apostle Paul gives instructions to Titus concerning the special way to help young people grow in their faith. He says:

Children are most affected by the lack of biblical principles lived out by their parents.

> *And you yourself must be an example to them by doing good works of every kind. Let everything you do reflect the integrity and seriousness of your teaching. Teach the truth so that your teaching can't be criticized. Then those who oppose us will be ashamed and have nothing bad to say about us* (Titus 2:7-8).

I'm convinced children, above all things, need living examples of what it means to follow Christ. As I think back on my childhood, the example of my father's walk with God is what motivated me Christ-ward. The way he talked, prayed and lived, demonstrated to me that God was real, the Bible was true, and that happiness would be mine if I followed that example. No, my Dad was not perfect—a point he repeatedly made very clear to us as children—but we knew that the God he loved and served was perfect and totally worthy of our faith and devotion. Dad continually pointed us to the right and true source of life. As proof of the effectiveness of his example and teaching, all six of us children have followed and served God.

Children need to grow up knowing a parent's love, care and protection. But more than that, they also need the biblical orientation that well-adjusted Christian parents can provide. I challenge you to make your home a happy and wonderful training center for your children. Give them the opportunity to grow up knowing the comfort, love and joy of a family where God is honored, trusted and obeyed. Surely this is the kind of environment God intended for all families. That's why He commanded us all to *"Honor your father and mother. Then you will live a long, full life in the land the Lord your God is giving you."*

THE SIXTH COMMANDMENT

You must not murder (Exodus 20:13).

With all the killings on TV, movies and video games, have we become desensitized to the value of human life?

Why does our world seem so enthralled with murder?

THE FIFTH COMMANDMENT in the old King James version of the Bible reads: *"Thou shalt not kill."* This has prompted many to take stands against any action that ends human life. However, the Hebrew word used that has been translated "kill" is *tirtzach,*[1] which means "assassinate." The particular meaning, then, has to do with "murder," or a senseless

---

[1] "Tirtzach" is the term used by Dr. Laura Schlessinger and Rabbi Stewart Vogel in their book *The Ten Commandments*, HarperCollins, New York, 2006, p. 186. Others, including Dr. Philip Ryken in his book, *Written in Stone*, use the Hebrew word "ratzach" meaning "the illegal killing of human beings."

killing, rather than putting an end to human life. This clarification should help us better understand distinctions the Bible makes between murder, the right to self-defense, the death penalty, and warfare in general. It further helps us deal with issues such as suicide, abortion, and euthanasia.

Murder is a contemptible thing. Rightly so, God has condemned this action in His commandments. Its evil, along with its consequences, is illustrated in a murder that took place in Bogota, Colombia, in 1948, dramatically changing the course of that entire nation.

The gruesome story begins the morning of April 9. Juan Roa closed the door of his small, rundown home in a suburb of Bogota and headed downtown. He was wearing a ragged brown suit, torn yellow shoes and a dirty felt hat. Hidden in his pocket was a gun.

His destination was the Agustin Nieto Building where Jorge Gaitan, a popular presidential candidate, had his law offices. Juan Roa arrived around 10 am. He found the site of Gaitan's office and took the elevator up to the tenth floor. He walked into the reception area and requested to see the presidential candidate. The receptionist politely explained that Gaitan was in a meeting and couldn't be disturbed. Juan Roa cursed, left the building, and hid in an area where he could plainly see the building's entrance.

Around noon, when Gaitan exited the building for lunch, Juan Roa jumped from his hiding place, fired three shots, and critically wounded Gaitan.

Horror stricken, pedestrians began shouting and chasing the murderer fleeing down the street. The mob caught up to Roa and began to beat him with rocks, sticks, and anything they could find They ripped off his clothes and pummeled him to death, literally tearing him limb from limb, leaving parts of his remains scattered down several streets.

As news spread of the fatal shooting, another crowd gathered at the hospital. When Gaitan's death was confirmed, the crowd turned angry and began marching toward the Presidential Palace. "Long live Colombia! Down with the *godos* [conservatives]!" they shouted. Thousands from all over the city joined the enraged mob. Soldiers of the presidential guard tried to disperse the demonstrators, but the crowd had grown so vast it was now impossible to control.

Liberal leaders in the crowd accused political conservatives with the death of Gaitan, and demanded revenge. In response, the crowd set fire to government buildings and city landmarks. Looters took advantage of the confusion and laid havoc on downtown stores and offices. A substantial portion of the city center was destroyed.

In response, several tanks and armored trucks approached the Bolivar Plaza where the largest concentration of the mob had gathered. Their commander, Captain Serpa, opened his tank hatch and tried to calm the situation and disperse the crowds. A sniper in the crowd, however, shot and killed the captain. The soldiers responded by opening fire on the people, killing hundreds and injuring thousands. The city was in complete chaos. Only the sector that surrounded the Presidential Palace remained under military control.

It was later discovered that members of the police force joined the uprising and equipped rioters with weapons. Violence spread throughout the country. Thousands who sought safety from random killers crowded into the cities, adding to the severe social unrest. The uncontrollable violence eventually ended in 1960 when political liberals and conservatives signed a peace pact. When all the dead were counted, it was determined that the murder of Jorge Gaitan resulted in the deaths of more than 400,000 people. The in-depth account is written in Colombia's history books under the title, La Violencia (The Violence).

But the account doesn't end there. Gaitán's assassination marked another beginning, one that sadly and dangerously persists to this very day. The act of murder by Juan Roa birthed the present-day guerrilla movements. Disgruntled revolutionaries took to the hills and began their reign of terror. The Revolutionary Armed Forces of Colombia (FARC), one of the globe's most brutal guerrilla groups, was born. This was followed by the Medellin Cartel, led by the ruthless drug-dealer, Pablo Escobar. Next came the National Liberation Army (ELN)—the most political of the rebel groups, which formed the powerful Cali Cartel.

In an effort to control all these revolutionary groups, the paramilitary army was created. However, it dealt its own cruel and infamous brand of "justice." All these groups together have added another 67,000 to the assassination records.

The Lord commands: *"You must not murder."*

The atrocity of ending a life

Life is the most precious and sacred gift God has given us. The fact we're made in His image grants every single person astounding potential, and indicates that everyone is extremely valuable. So much so, that God alone has the right to end life.

To murder is to commit a savage, perverse and diabolic act against God. The murderer reduces human life to the rank of animals and he himself becomes a monster. The horrors seen in Colombia provide an example. The unfortunate reality is that as we look around in the world, no society is free from similar atrocities. Murder has become so commonplace it often is the lead story on our news, as well as in our conversations. How deplorable.

Life no longer is considered sacred. Today, it seems, there's more public outrage for killing a cat or dog than a person. Violence has popped out from our TV screens and walks around in our streets. To protect ourselves we build fences, put bars on our doors and windows, install alarm systems, and buy guns.

God's commandment is clear and concise: *"You must not murder."*

Life represents the eternal link that exists between people and the Creator. It demands respect of every life, simply because people bear the stamp of God's image. People are His exceptional property. When a human life is taken, a direct attack against God has taken place. For this reason, this commandment gives human life dignity; it explains our particular importance.

As we view each one of the commandments, we recognize they deal with the various aspects of the quality of life God has given us. Knowing who we are as God's creation permits us to understand why we're not to commit adultery, not to steal, not to testify falsely, not to covet, and not to murder.

Applying the commandment

In order for us to carefully implement this commandment today, it's important to understand how it was interpreted by the ancient Jews. In Exodus 20:13 the command is stated: *"You must not murder."* In Exodus 21:12-14 we're told how the Israelites were to apply the commandment:

> *Anyone who assaults and kills another person must be put to death. But if it was simply an accident permitted by God, I will appoint a place of refuge where the slayer can run for safety [cities of refuge, Numbers 35]. However,*

if someone deliberately kills another person, then the slayer must be dragged even from my altar and be put to death.

Exodus 21:15-25 goes into even more detail based on the Old Testament guide of *"an eye for an eye and a tooth for a tooth."* As we read through these verses, we understand it's God who formed the rules to conserve and govern human life. Based on these verses we see He was the one who established capital punishment. In Genesis 9:6 He explains the reason: *"If anyone takes a human life, that person's life will also be taken by human hands. For God made human beings in his own image."*

Because of the sacred origin of life and its eternal significance, the unwarranted taking of a human life is to be punished. The offender's own life is to be taken. Clearly, God has imposed the death penalty. Therefore, to disallow capital punishment is to belittle both the significance of life as well as the Giver of life. At the same time, the declarations in Exodus 21 show God requires justice and introduces impartial rules to decide the gravity of each case.

Life represents the eternal link that exists between people and the Creator.

God's law further puts limits on revenge. For instance, if a man lost an eye during a fight, he wasn't allowed to decapitate his aggressor in revenge. Exodus 21:23 explains the maximum revenge allowed would be *"an eye for an eye and a tooth for a tooth."* Revenge could never exceed the injury inflicted.

Murder, then, calls for maximum punishment. It's not only the greatest public offense imaginable, but a blow to the face of the Creator who gave it. Because God demands it, it's irresponsible to let a criminal live so he can kill again.

Paul says governments are God's instrument to carry out justice on earth.

Furthermore, Romans 13:3-4 shows us that our respective governments are the chosen agents to punish criminals:

> For the authorities do not strike fear in people who are acting right, but in those who are doing wrong. Would you want to live without fear of the authorities? Do what is right, and they will honor you. The authorities are God's servants, sent for your good. But if you are doing wrong, of course you should be afraid, for they have the power to punish you. They are God's servants, sent for the very purpose of punishing those who do what is wrong.

According to Paul, governments are God's instrument to carry out justice on earth. Referring to the authority and rights given civic authorities, Paul, talking about a magistrate, adds: *"He does not bear the sword for nothing"* (Romans 13:4, NIV). Paul adds that this divine right makes the government the *"agent of wrath to bring punishment on the wrongdoer."* Every government is therefore charged with protecting the innocent as well as punishing criminals according to the seriousness of the crime.

Jesus and civil authority

Jesus is our example. The way He accepted His capture in the Garden of Gethsemane models the respect we ought to give police and civil servants. Though the soldiers representing the government (the "civil sword," as separate from the "private" or "personal sword") were unjustly serving the interests of Jewish leaders, He nevertheless showed respect for them. He demonstrated the way people should submit to civil authority. Jesus' remarks to Pilate explain the reason: *"You would have no power over me at all unless it were given to you from above"* (John 19:11).

We find an interesting side-road by observing how Jesus reacted when Peter cut off the ear of one of the soldiers. Jesus said to Peter, *"Put your sword back into its sheath. Shall I not drink from the cup of suffering the Father has given me?"* (John 18:11). Note the two "swords" present: Peter's (representing an instrument of personal protection) and the soldier's (representing the government's instrument of God-given power). Interestingly, Jesus didn't tell Peter to get rid of his personal sword, but simply to put it away in respect for the civic sword that was present.

The fact is we're surprised to learn that Peter was even carrying a sword. This leads us to ask, "Were the other disciples armed as well?" In Luke 22:48-49 we are told: *"When the other disciples saw what was about to happen, they exclaimed, 'Lord, should we fight? We brought the swords!'"* Obviously, Peter wasn't alone in wanting to protect Jesus. Further, it's safe to assume that if carrying a sword had been inappropriate, Jesus surely would have forbidden it much earlier.

And one more side-road: some say Jesus never used force to carry out his work. But in John 2:13-16 we find some rather forceful, if not in fact, violent actions:

> *It was nearly time for the Jewish Passover celebration, so Jesus went to Jerusalem. In the Temple area he saw merchants selling cattle, sheep, and doves for sacrifices; he also saw dealers at tables exchanging foreign money. Jesus made a whip from some ropes and chased them all out of the Temple. He drove out the sheep and cattle, scattered the money changers' coins over the floor, and turned over their tables. Then, going over to the people who sold doves, he told them, "Get these things out of here. Stop turning my Father's house into a marketplace!"*

Jesus' reaction to the abuses in His *"Father's house"* must have been quite confrontational, otherwise the culprits wouldn't have scattered as they did. This should help us understand that God is angered by man's offensive behavior and never accepts it.

In this connection, let's look at the incident found in John 18:33-38, the conversation between Pilate and Jesus:

> Then Pilate went back into his headquarters and called for Jesus to be brought to him. "Are you the king of the Jews?" he asked him. Jesus replied, "Is this your own question, or did others tell you about me?" "Am I a Jew?" Pilate retorted. "Your own people and their leading priests brought you to me for trial. Why? What have you done?" Jesus answered, "My Kingdom is not an earthly kingdom. If it were, my followers would fight to keep me from being handed over to the Jewish leaders. But my Kingdom is not of this world."

What does Jesus mean when He talks about His kingdom and His followers not fighting? Some argue that Jesus was against the use of all military force and that Christians should never take up arms. I believe Jesus was saying something very different. When He said, *"My Kingdom is not an earthly kingdom. If it were, my followers would fight,"* He was not making a statement on war, rather saying Christianity is not spread by force, as the Moors spread Islam throughout northern Africa, or like the Crusades, or the Spaniard's attempt to convert Indians in Colonial times. Christians conquer the world through love and peace. Our "armies" don't use rifles, missiles, or bombs.

Rather we proclaim the greatness and the truthfulness of the Gospel through lives that have been radically transformed by the incomparable power of the Gospel message.

The right to self defense

Because the Bible is our guide, we're to measure all our concepts and ideas by what it teaches. If our conclusions fall in line with its teachings, then we know we're on the right path. If they don't, we must discard them. Based on this premise, I believe the Bible teaches we have a right to self-defense.

I have several friends who are pacifists. They like to quote Matthew 5:39-44, *"If someone slaps you on the right cheek, offer the other cheek also"*—a reading that they believe is the ultimate proof for support of their pacifist arguments. They also cite Romans 12:17, *"Never pay back evil with more evil. Do things in such a way that everyone can see you are honorable,"* as well as Proverbs 25:21-22, *"If your enemies are hungry, give them food to eat. If they are thirsty, give them water to drink. You will heap burning coals on their heads, and the LORD will reward you."*

When Paul's life was threatened by Jewish leaders he didn't turn the other cheek.

My answer is that for a proper biblical perspective, all the Bible verses on this subject need to be considered. This is where passages dealing with our right to self-defense come in. For instance, when Paul's life was threatened by Jewish leaders he didn't turn the other cheek, instead he defended himself by appealing to Caesar (Acts 25:11). Of course, we can quote Jesus when He said to *"turn the other cheek."* But we must also remember that He told the disciples: *"If you don't have a sword, sell your cloak and buy one!"* (Luke 22:36). And He said this to them during the Last Supper, when telling them about His impending crucifixion. It seems clear Jesus was warning them of the troubles to come and their right to self-defense.

In this connection, let me tell you about Fulvio Morris, a pastor I met during one of our pastor conferences in Uruguay. He was a student in our distance Bible School and sensed God had called him to take the Gospel to the inner city of Montevideo. He remembered there was an old church right in the heart of the district that would make an ideal ministry headquarters.

Fulvio and his wife visited the abandoned church and saw there was a place in the building that, while they refurbished the neglected church, could be turned into their home. After obtaining the necessary permits, they moved in. However, because of the criminal element in the area, Fulvio wisely took a gun for protection.

The neighbors were amazed at the couple's courage, particularly because Fulvio was short and small statured and his wife a thin little thing. They were no match for the tough gangs that ruled the streets around them.

After a few days in their new home, Fulvio discovered that delinquents were using the church property as an escape route from the police. He got a group of young men from other churches to help him and they built a wall around the back of the church, blocking off the escape route. This, however, angered the street thugs and they decided to retaliate.

A few nights after putting up the wall, Fulvio and his wife were awakened by someone breaking into the church. Fulvio grabbed his gun and slipped silently down the stairs, his wife hanging on to him for dear life. He snuck around behind the thugs and jumped out with his gun drawn. "Freeze!" he shouted. Seeing the gun, those furthest away took off running, but Fulvio was able to corner one of them. He asked his trembling wife to call the police.

The Bible gives us our parameters: rights do have limits.

While he waited with his cornered prisoner—arms up in the air—, Fulvio began to preach to him: "Look at you, a young man starting out and already a criminal. You should be ashamed of yourself. You're ruining your life," he chided. "If you don't change, you'll end up rotting in prison. What's worse, one day you're going to have to face God. If you don't get right with Him, you'll spend eternity in hell." His sermon continued, "I want you to know there's a better way. One filled with joy and peace and love, a new kind of life only Jesus can give…" And Fulvio preached away, holding him at gunpoint, until the police arrived.

By the next day, news had spread about the little preacher brave enough to stand up to the thugs. Curious, people began coming to the run-down church, and along with them came some of the local thieves, drug addicts, and prostitutes. A wonderful church ministry began which, as far as I know, continues to this day.

Was Fulvio wrong in protecting himself and his wife with a gun? What would have happened had he not had a gun? Was Fulvio right to use his gun to keep the delinquent cornered while he preached to him and waited for the police? Wasn't the little preacher with a gun in his hand what created the curiosity that brought people to church to hear the Gospel?

Of course, a story like this merely illustrates a point; it doesn't establish doctrine. In Exodus 22:2-3, however, God gives clear instructions about the right to defend both home and property: *"If a thief is caught in the act of breaking into a house and is struck and killed in the process, the person who killed the thief is not guilty of murder. But if it happens in daylight, the one who killed the thief is guilty of murder."*

Along with the right to self-defense, the Bible gives us our parameters: rights do have limits. In this case, if someone comes to steal from us at night—in the dark when we can't see—and we kill that person, it's a God-given right. However, the same right doesn't come into play during daytime, when we can see the attacker and identify him (the assumption here is a non-life threatening situation). At that point we let the law take over his judgment. In other words, the life of every human—good or bad—is sacred. God asks us to do everything in our power to preserve each life— even that of a criminal—because it's human and has enormous spiritual value to God.

Can God be accused of being an assassin?

The Bible recounts massive killings ordered by God. Does that mean we can accuse Him of being a mass murderer? Some who criticize the God of the Bible seem to think so!

Does God have a right to punish what He has created?

We established earlier that the sixth commandment refers to killing someone unjustly. Some accuse God of doing just that when He ordered the flood (Genesis 6), or the destruction of men, women and children in Sodom and Gomorrah (Genesis 19), or when He commanded the Israelites to destroy the Amalekites, including the elderly, and women and children (Deuteronomy 25:19). The same point can be made when He ordered the death of Achan and his family (Joshua 7), and of Ananias and Sapphira (Acts 5).

Were these killings justified? Did God break His

own commandment? These examples can be difficult to understand, so let's dig in. Theologically speaking, these deaths all fall under what are called "God's acts of retribution," meaning He's enacting just punishment for human rebellion, disobedience and sin. Does God have a right to punish what He has created? Some would deny Him that right. However, we read in Isaiah 1:24: *"Therefore, the Lord, the Lord of Heaven's Armies, the Mighty One of Israel, says, I will take revenge on my enemies and pay back my foes!"* The Bible is very clear that God, as Creator and Judge, can enact judgment any time His laws have been transgressed. Take the Flood, for example. In Genesis 6 we read:

> *The LORD observed the extent of human wickedness on the earth, and he saw that everything they thought or imagined was consistently and totally evil. So the LORD was sorry he had ever made them and put them on the earth. It broke his heart. And the LORD said, "I will wipe this human race I have created from the face of the earth. Yes, and I will destroy every living thing—all the people, the large animals, the small animals that scurry along the ground, and even the birds of the sky. I am sorry I ever made them"* (Genesis 6:5-7).

Likewise, God warned Abraham about Sodom and Gomorrah's pending doom: *"So the LORD told Abraham, 'I have heard a great outcry from Sodom and Gomorrah, because their sin is so flagrant'"* (Genesis

18:20). So grievous and generalized was their sin that when Abraham interceded for the righteous, God responded that He wouldn't destroy the city if He found ten good people (Genesis 18:23-33). You know the story; not even ten righteous people could be found in the entire city. His divine actions were justified.

God is the author of life, and only He has the right to order how every life should end.

What about the killing of the inhabitants of Palestine during Joshua's conquest? Was it justifiable for God to order the death of men, women and children, the elderly, and even animals, thus erasing entire tribes from the face of the earth? God was enacting punishment as foretold to Abraham in Genesis 15:13-16:

> Then the LORD told Abram, "You can be sure that your descendants will be strangers in a foreign land [Egypt], where they will be oppressed as slaves for 400 years. But I will punish the nation that enslaves them, and in the end they will come away with great wealth [exodus]. (As for you, you will die in peace, at a ripe old age.) After four generations your descendants will return here to this land, for the sins of the Amorites do not yet warrant their destruction.

It appears there's a line that, once crossed, brings about God's judgment. This is a very scary and awesome thought! Crossing that line can bring swift and devastating consequences. The sinfulness and depravity of the Amorites had become so great, God used the armies of Israel to bring them to judgment.[2] Actually, every single death comes as a consequence of God's judgment on sin. God told Adam and Eve in the Garden of Eden: "If you eat its fruit, you are sure to die" (Genesis 2:17). Paul explains that this is the reason all people die: "When Adam sinned, sin entered the world. Adam's sin brought death, so death spread to everyone, for everyone sinned" (Romans 5:12).

Abortion

Much has been said, written and preached about abortion. Let's remind ourselves of the biblical principles that define our conclusions.

As I've carefully tried to point out, God is the author of life, and only He has the right to order how every life should end. When we pause long enough to consider that every pregnancy is the result of God's creation of a new life, we realize that abortion is the human act of putting to an end a life God has created. Genetic science shows that life begins at conception, and we read that "God created everything through [our Lord Jesus], and nothing was created except through him" (John 1:3). Therefore, whether we take life away before or after birth, it's still murder. Since abortion is killing someone to whom God has given

---

[5] Similar incidents are found in Deuteronomy 18:9-13; 9:5-7; 7:8; Numbers 33:55-56; 2Thessalonians 1:8. Additional texts giving reason for God's judgments are Isaiah 61:2; 63:4; Jeremiah 46:10; Ezekiel 25:14; and Psalm 94:1.

life, before trying to excuse it based on a woman's rights, we should begin by first considering the higher rights that belong to God the life-giver.

Exodus 21:22-23 indicates that the fetus is protected under the divine laws of retribution:

> Now suppose two men are fighting, and in the process they accidentally strike a pregnant woman so she gives birth prematurely. If no further injury results, the man who struck the woman must pay the amount of compensation the woman's husband demands and the judges approve. But if there is further injury [in other words, the baby dies], the punishment must match the injury: a life for a life...

The fact that a fetus cannot survive outside the uterus for several months would seem to tell us it obviously deserves the same protection in a mother's womb before birth as it legally receives after birth. Legalizing abortion is to directly defy everything the Bible says about the origin and value of life itself.

Suicide

Of all murders the most incomprehensible is suicide. Taking one's own life most certainly violates God's commandment. I consider suicide a cowardly and selfish act which leaves huge emotional scars and burdens on relatives and loved ones. The person who kills himself/herself tries to escape a personal problem without considering the immensely magnified burden for those left behind. It's a terrible and devastating act.

Does a person go to hell for self-murder? It can most certainly lead to eternal damnation. In ancient times it was thought that because the person had no time to confess his sins, he would go immediately to hell. However, if the entrance to heaven depends on remembering and confessing every sin, we all have serious problems at death. What leads us to heaven aren't the good things we've done before we die, but what Christ has done on our behalf. When Jesus died on the cross, He paid the price for all our sins. He has assured eternal life for all who be-lieve in Him.

I consider suicide a cowardly and selfish act which leaves huge emotional scars.

I'm reminded of Dr. Edward John Carnell, a great Bible scholar, whose books inspired many of us who sought Biblical truth during our college days. Carnell served as the President of Fuller Seminary in California. Sadly, because of theo-logical differences in the seminary, Carnell became the subject of much criticism. He fell into deep depression and apparently died of a self-induced drug overdose. How do we explain that? His testimony, thinking and written work demonstrate that he was a true son of God. I believe one day I'll see Edward Carnell in heaven and be able to thank him for his contributions to my walk with God.

"Suicide," says Dr. J.I. Packer, "is the act of a mind

unhinged; though such acts do not of themselves forfeit God's grace, as was once thought, yet suicide is a direct breach of God's command."[3]

How people in some cultures support and promote the practice of suicide bombers totally baffles me. For a person to cover himself with explosives and go out and kill himself, while at the same time taking with him as many of his hated enemy as possible, is beyond my understanding. The fact that these actions represent the beliefs of large sects of people is simply inconceivable. To think of hatred so strong that people from early childhood are taught to die this way by parents, teachers and sect leaders is nightmarish.

No matter the motivations, no matter the politics, God still says: *"You must not murder."*

Euthanasia

The idea that a patient or the patient's family might request medical assistance to end his or her life, is a concept introduced by Dr. Jack Kevorkian. The purpose of "assisted suicide" for terminally ill patients is to end their pain and suffering, as well as the high cost of hospitals, physicians and medication.

However, this sixth commandment condemns the concept. It may seem like a logical solution to end the pain and desperation of elderly people and others who wish to end their lives regardless of the situation, but such induced death is still murder. People may compare it to ending the life of an injured animal or

---

[3] J.I. Packer, *The Ten Commandments,* Tyndale House, Wheaton, IL., 1982, p. 53.

letting the vet put a cat or dog to sleep, but there is a great difference between a person and an animal. Euthanasia is morally unacceptable to God. We don't have the right to play God. Only He decides when to end the life of a person He created in His own image.

What about those who are kept alive with machines, by so-called "heroic measures"? A person may be kept alive by man-made machinery, but once the equipment has been turned off, it's God who decides when the person dies. Shutting off machinery and allowing the death of a person who's been uncon- scious for some time with no hopes of recovery doesn't constitute euthanasia. On the contrary, it's allowing a person to die with dignity. The difficulty is in deciding when to disconnect the equipment. Normally the decision is made when the doctor and loved ones realize there's no hope of the patient recovering.

What about war?

I believe the subject of the rightness or wrongness of war was simpler centuries ago when weapons of war were much more primitive. People still died, of course, but not nearly in such massive and devastating ways. Today, however, the world's weapons of mass destruc- tion—nuclear, biological, chemical and radiological weapons—have the capacity to destroy our entire planet. This leads to terrible thoughts and fears. What can we do to protect ourselves? Is it even right to try?

When we study the Pentateuch and the history of

Israel, it's clear that God allowed his people to protect themselves from their enemies. In fact, from such examples (as well as those in the New Testament) we derive the concept of "just wars."

The problem with any type of war is the resulting toll on innocent lives.

God taught Cain (Genesis 4) that we're *"our brother's keeper."* This same idea is repeated by Jesus when He tells us to love our neighbor. Implicit in these orders is the fact that we're to protect the helpless.

When we refuse to help someone who's being attacked we go against the teachings given us in the parable of the Good Samaritan (Luke 10). Jesus used this parable to define how we're to love our neighbor. We can even apply these same principles when we see a weak nation attacked by a stronger, despicable oppressor whose intent is to cause great damage. It's this type of thinking that has led Christians to speak of "just wars," that is, coming to the defense of a nation being attacked unjustly by a ruthless one. (Saint Augustine was the first to reach this conclusion back in the fourth century.)

Let's take World War II as an example. We remember Hitler's evil intentions. The Nazis believed they were a superior race and proceeded to exterminate Jews. Eventually this led to the terrible Second World War. For the sake of argument, if we transport ourselves to those times, what would be our responsibility toward the less powerful nations of Europe and toward the Jews who were burned by the thousands in the ovens of Auschwitz, Dachau, Treblinka, Buchenwald, and Mauthausen? Were free nations to do nothing? Surely to do nothing would have been to act like the priest or the Levite in the Parable of the Good Samaritan.

It was this type of reasoning that resulted in the creation of the United Nations: free governments determining that by standing together they'd stop the rise of other Hitler-like leaders. The idea was further developed and refined, and the result was the concept of "preventive wars," that is, when a government attempts to overpower or conquer a weaker one, it's appropriate to attack the threatening government before it reaches its goal. This was the idea behind the United State's controversial attack on the abusive and criminal Iraqi dictator, Saddam Hussein.

The problem with any type of war is the resulting toll on innocent lives. For instance, during World War II, 20 million Russians perished and six million Jews were exterminated; six and one half million Germans died; as well as one million Allied troops. Further, defending our ideals gave excuse to develop stronger and more potent weapons of defense. The atomic bomb dropped by the U.S. on Hiroshima killed 70,000 men, women and children instantly. President Truman defended using the two atomic bombs against Japan because they brought the war in the Pacific to a quick end and saved the lives of thousands of U.S. soldiers.

There is yet another problem. In our modern

world there's a lack of impartial reporting. There are numerous news agencies, each representing different political interests, especially today regarding the con-

As Christians, how are we to reconcile our varied ideas on the subject of war?

flict in the Middle East. Arab agencies such as Al-Jazeera, are constantly portraying the U.S. and Israel in a bad light. American news networks seek to defend the interests of the U.S. and Israel, thus reporting on the atrocities committed by Arabs. But are our news agencies completely unbiased? Can we believe all the news that's being reported to us? Surely there are details missing from both sides. Distorted ideas can lead to very dangerous actions. Let's not forget that war is terrible and all sides are responsible in one way or another.

As Christians, how are we to reconcile our several and varied ideas on the subject of war? Can we justify so many deaths? When modern weapons cause so much destruction of life, what should our stance be on "just wars"? What about the teaching that we really are our brothers' guardians? Does loving our neighbor justify going to war? How can we live up to the spirit of Leviticus 19:16: *"Do not stand idly by when your neighbor's life is threatened."* [4]

Modern wars are difficult to defend. When we think about all the weaponry that's been invented to kill thousands at a time, it seems impossible for us to

---

[4] Special translation of this text used by Dr. Laura Schlessinger in *Los Diez Mandamientos*, HarperCollins Publishers, 2006, p. 195.

approve, much less participate, in such terrible activity. At the same time, we must also understand that those same weapons can be used against us, destroying our loved ones, our possessions, our towns and cities, and our nation.

What if we do nothing? What if we let the evil people in the world raise havoc without lifting a finger to stop them? What would the world be like if Hitler, Genghis Khan, Mussolini, or Abd-er Rahman (described ahead) had been successful in their terrible plans? What would happen if the government of Colombia stopped fighting the FARC? What if one of the ruthless guerrilla leaders became their president? What if Peru were governed by the *Sendero Luminoso* (Shining Path)? Would these criminals and assassins turn into decent people overnight? What would happen to our world if just and righteous rulers no longer ran for office?

Does loving our neighbor justify going to war?

As for me, I'd like to think I could turn the other cheek and let evil people do me harm. If they took my shirt, I could give them another one. If they demanded it, I'd go the extra mile. But there's much more at stake. If the issue were just me, then I'd put up with a lot. However, I have a wife, children, and grandchildren. I have friends, a home, a neighborhood, a city, a state, a nation. What's my God-given duty and responsibility to all that surrounds me in this world?

Would it be correct to turn the other cheek and allow others to hurt my wife, my children and grandchildren, my neighbors, my hometown without attempting to defend them? Is that what the Lord means when He tells us *"never pay back evil with more evil"* (Romans 12:17)? The point is that in many cases it's not my personal cheek I'm out to defend, but rather the cheeks of those I love more than life itself. I wouldn't be trying to pay back evil with more evil, rather defending all that's good and right, just and decent.

It's not correct to assume that no good has come out of war. Our western civilization would have perished in the Eighth Century had it not been for the Battle of Tours (732 A.D.). At that time the Muslims ruled Spain, and under the command of Abd-er Rahman, these Muslims went out and conquered northern Africa, Egypt and Syria. They then decided to invade Western Europe and destroy Christianity. The Muslim army, with 400,000 men, crossed the Pyrenees and reached the Loire River in central France. There, French troops led by Charles Martel fought to the death for their homes and beliefs. After a fierce 10-day battle, the French killed Abd-er Rahman. Without a leader, the Muslims turned tail and returned to Spain. Had it not been for Charles Martel and his valiant, self-sacrificing soldiers fighting for Christian rights, you and I today might have been Muslims.

Speaking of wars, it was the Civil War in the U.S. that resulted in the abolition of slavery. Neo-paganism would control all of Europe if Hitler hadn't been defeated. Peru would be under the command of the *Sendero Luminoso* (Shining Path guerrillas) if the battles of September 1992 hadn't resulted in the capture of Abimael Guzman. Similarly, Colombia today enjoys a freedom that once escaped the nation, because a President and his army have determined to dethrone the terrorist FARC, the ELN and the paramilitary forces.

As Christians we must address these issues that have to do with life and death, self-defense, abortion, suicide, euthanasia and war. Each represents a subject that directly or indirectly affects us. Just think what life would be like in your town if there were no police, no judges, no state government, no armed forces to defend your personal rights and interests, much less those of the entire nation. That's why each Christian must consider the implications of these subjects and reach appropriate ethical and biblical conclusions. Remember that when Jesus asks us to love as He has loved us, it doesn't mean we should love the sins of those who are evil. Yes, we must love our neighbor, but love Him within the boundaries of what God loves and what God rejects and punishes.

Our inner potential

As I conclude this chapter, I must underline one more teaching Jesus gave us on the subject of homicide, a subject that has to do with all the potential in our hearts. We may not feel like murderers, but Christ tells us:

You have heard that our ancestors were told,
'You must not murder. If you commit murder,
you are subject to judgment.' But I say, if you
are even angry with someone, you are subject to
judgment! If you call someone an idiot, you are
in danger of being brought before the court. And
if you curse someone, you are in danger of the
fires of hell (Matthew 5:21-22).

By now it should be clear to us that each commandment makes internal as well as external claims. With the sixth commandment we see that building up resentment and hatred in our hearts culminates in potential homicide.

I remember a dreadful call I received from my brother-in-law, pastor of a Christian and Missionary Alliance church in California. He told me his 68-year-old mother (my mother-in-law) had been raped by a 22-year-old man: "When I learned what that pervert had done to Mom, my heart filled with uncontrollable hatred. For the first time I realized that, as a Christian and a minister, I was capable of taking another's life.

Building up resentment and hatred in our hearts culminates in potential homicide.

The prospect terrified me. In my heart I was no better than the man who had done this to Mom. I had to ask God to forgive me and help me overcome my hatred."

When someone hurts us, we easily fall into what

John Calvin called "homicide of the heart." We must ask God to deliver us from bitterness, resentment, and any desire for vengeance. If we allow any of these feelings to grow in our hearts, who knows what the consequences will be?

So it is that this commandment, along with each of the previous ones, challenges us to examine our hearts and our devotion to God. This one should make every one of us especially appreciative of God's wonderful gift of life. May each of us, under God, make the best of life and truly enjoy it to the fullest.

THE SEVENTH COMMANDMENT

You must not commit adultery (Exodus 20:14).

Because we possess such powerful sex drives, are we truly made to be faithful to just one person?

Why does God make exclusive love within marriage so important?

I SUSPECT there's never been a town or a community that's been immune to the problem of adultery. What's worse, many today believe the seventh commandment is completely out of date. God, they rationalize, must not have fully understood the nature of man when he demanded, *"You must not commit adultery."* With Sigmund Freud and our hedonistic society, many believe that fulfilling one's sex drive is the most important part of life. Placing restrictions on its fulfillment is ludicrous.

Thinking back to some of my childhood, I realize now that my opposition to this commandment surfaced quite early in life. My older sister loved the game of "wedding." Whenever a group of us got together, she'd separate us into couples. I often had to play the part of a groom. Sometimes it wasn't so bad because I liked some of the girls. Other times I wanted to annul the marriage even before we walked down the aisle.

During one of those games, my sister tried to get me to "marry" a girl named Martha. I told her, "I already married her once and I don't like her anymore. This time I want to marry Julia." My sister agreed and the game went on with another bride.

Of course, it was just an innocent, childhood game. But as I think back on it, it sounds far too familiar to the comments I hear from married adults. The sanctity of marriage is truly on shaky ground today. One of the most devastating culprits is adultery. According to Americans for Divorce Reform, 38 percent of married couples in 2005 divorced. There's nothing playful about such an alarming statistic. Think of all the broken promises, lost dreams, and hurting people. It's much like the game I played back in Cuba. Those married to their "Marthas" have decided to leave them because they now want their "Julias." It doesn't matter what God says, or what happens to all the "Marthas" or the people involved. The important thing is to find happiness for oneself, even if it means destroying our present family.

But God says: *"You must not commit adultery."*

What's behind the commandment? I really don't know how to discuss this commandment without relating it to marriage. It seems to me that the primary reason God gave it was to protect the sanctity of marriage. Back at the very beginning—in Genesis 2—when God created marriage, He said: *"It is not good for the man to be alone. I will make a helper who is just right for him."* And the Scripture adds: *"Then the Lord God made a woman... and he brought her to the man... This explains why a man leaves his father and mother and is joined to his wife, and the two are united into one."* The picture is one of monogamous marriage; one man and one wife in lasting union, or "until death do us part."

The sanctity of marriage is truly on shaky ground today.

But in today's world we're not interested in this prohibition. Instead we ask, "Could it be that God doesn't understand the very creature He created? Doesn't He see how unhappy some marriages are? Doesn't He understand sexual frustration? Doesn't He sympathize with our need for change and variety? Doesn't He see that 'Martha' is getting old and losing her shape, and that 'Julia' is young, beautiful, more understanding, and much more passionate? Doesn't God want me to be happy?"

Of course God knows. Of course He sees. Nothing

is hidden from His eyes: *"The Lord sees every heart and knows every plan and thought"* (1Chronicles 28:9). *"He knows what lies hidden in darkness,"* adds Daniel 2:22. In addition, what's extremely hard for us to learn is another bit of information regarding God: *"My thoughts are nothing like your thoughts,"* says the Lord, *"and my ways are far beyond anything you could imagine"* (Isaiah 55:8). And, to cite one more verse, we learn the plans God has for us *"are plans for good and not for disaster"* (Jeremiah 29:11). Rather than being turned off by this commandment, let's assume these statements about God are true and endeavor to find out why this Seventh Commandment is good, fair and just.

Seriously, what's the purpose of this commandment?

Each time someone commits adultery he or she is defying one of God's primary principles of life: that is, faithfulness. As we've noted, God created marriage because the experience of "loneliness" is unique to man. Animals fulfill their purpose by just being animals. Man, on the other hand, is much more complex and represents much more than mere existence and instincts. Every person, irrespective of race or background, has incredible potential simply because he's been made in the image of God. Unlike animals, however, any person can fall far short of his potential.

How can a person achieve his maximum potential? First off, God says it isn't good to do it alone; we need a companion. Man (and I use the term generically, referring to "man and woman") was never intended to be a self-contained being wandering about the planet. He needs a partner, a companion—someone who perfectly complements him. Is it possible to be perfectly fulfilled when one is all wrapped up in oneself and one's wants? That's why God said: *"I will make a helper who is just right for him."* What the man lacked, the woman supplied. Contrary to

> *God created marriage because the experience of loneliness is unique to man.*

what Freud and others have tried to stuff into our heads, man's greatest, long-range need is for true, satisfying companionship, a faithful partner. Sex, as it were, is a wonderful fringe benefit, but not the essence of marriage. Because of the way God made us, our true nature comes out in the company of the helper who's just right for us:

> *While the man slept, the Lord God took out one of the man's ribs and closed up the opening. Then the Lord God made a woman from the rib, and he brought her to the man.[1] "At last!" the man exclaimed. "This one is bone from my bone, and flesh from my flesh! She will be called 'woman,' because she was taken from 'man.'" This explains why a man leaves his father and mother and is joined to his wife, and the two are united into one (Genesis 2:21-24).*

---

[1] Notice he did not create another man! God very clearly condemns homosexuality (Leviticus 18:22; 20:13; Romans 1:26-32).

Think how little has changed in our behavior since Adam stood in awe before this perfect new creature God had made for him. Whenever a pretty woman walks by a man she intuitively draws his attention. God's purpose when he created woman, however, wasn't to make a man become instinctively attracted to her, like animals do. Rather, His plan was to bring a man and woman together into a special, helping, completing, and lasting relationship—what we call marriage. In God's wonderful forethought He created woman especially for man. She wasn't created just to perform certain functions that make man momentarily happy. Not at all! She was created like man, in the image and likeness of God, intended to become his *alter ego*, his "other self." Together, as husband and wife, they become complete. They're intended to grow into a relationship that melds into a loving, productive, useful unit: *"the two are united into one."*

God has established that the goal of the sexual relationship is to unite two people into one.

For all these reasons and more, a casual sexual encounter between a man and a woman who aren't married is wrong. It shatters God's purpose, it debases the whole intent. As the Apostle Paul states: *"And don't you realize that if a man joins himself to a prostitute, he becomes one body with her? For the Scriptures say, 'The two are united into one'"* (1Corinthians 6:16).

God has established that the goal of the sexual relationship is to unite two people into one. An adulterous relationship makes a lie out of God's intention; it betrays what marriage is all about. God has designed sex as the pleasurable union that results in long-lasting love, fidelity, devotion, and commitment between a man and a woman. This beautiful relationship and happy union not only erases loneliness, but is important for the stability of a home, the health of children, and the building of a strong community.

As I see it, God's purpose for marriage is to create a union which encompasses the heart, soul and body of a man and a woman. Such a partnership produces: (1) indestructible companionship, (2) total emotional devotion, (3) intimate physical satisfaction, and (4) the acceptance needed by both the man and the woman to fulfill themselves as human beings. In this way marriage becomes a reflection of the love and oneness that exists in the Holy Trinity. God the Father, God the Son and God the Holy Spirit are eternally present in a partnership of inexplicable joy, communion and mutual satisfaction. That's our perfect model.

The way we destroy God's plan

Think of the beauty of the multiple and traditional vows a couple makes before God and man:

- I take you as my wife/husband,
- I promise to love you,
- I promise to honor you,

- I promise to keep you,
- I promise to serve you,
- I promise to care for you in sickness and in health,
- I promise to stick with you whether rich or poor,
- I promise to be faithful,
- I promise to forsake all others until death do us part.[2]

Adultery blatantly and in one grand sweep wipes out all of these promises. It makes a mockery of marriage and the vows taken. It cancels out the trust and confidence upon which it was based. It destroys what God was building: that *the two* would be *united into one*.

While God condemns adultery, he doesn't condemn sex. God isn't prudish. He doesn't blush nor hide His face when we mention the subject. God created sex! He made it for the pleasure and enjoyment of a man and a woman! However, He also set the rules. He knew how easily we can abuse this great gift, and for this reason He gave very clear instructions. His intention from the beginning was that our sexuality be enjoyed within the boundaries of marriage. Following God's plan gives a man and a woman the immense pleasure and joy that comes with His gift. The proof is found in the very heart of the Bible where, in the *Song of Songs*, God pro-

God's plan gives a man and a woman the immense pleasure and joy that comes with His gift.

---

[2] Interestingly, some manuals omit or tone down the last phrase. It seems as if no one expects that vow to be kept and therefore there's no point in asking the couple to lie to each other.

THE TEN COMMANDMENTS

vides us with His matrimonial manual, an incomparable guide to the pure pleasures of sex. He also talks
about it in other places of the Bible, for example,
Proverbs 5:18-19:

> *Let your wife be a fountain of blessing for you.*
> *Rejoice in the wife of your youth.*
> *She is a loving deer, a graceful doe.*
> *Let her breasts satisfy you always.*
> *May you always be captivated by her love.*

Then a warning follows in verses 20-21:

> *Why be captivated, my son, by an immoral woman,*
> *or fondle the breasts of a promiscuous woman?*
> *For the Lord sees clearly what a man does,*
> *examining every path he takes.*

Why do we mortals insist on breaking His rules?
Why do we knowingly and willingly do what we
know is wrong? Do we honestly think God is wrong
and we're right? Have our sexual impulses so blinded
us that we can't learn from all the failed and destroyed
marriages around us? Why do we deceive ourselves in
thinking our sin will have a different ending, that we
won't end up at the same dead end?

Adultery is to turn our backs on God

It's incredible that so many believe the Bible's teachings
about sex are obsolete and out of date. The public's
disregard for the Bible's teachings is evident in what is
said in magazines, heard on the radio, seen on television,
and displayed in advertisements. The message is

blatant and insistent: sex is for everyone's enjoyment anytime, anyplace. It's good for relaxation, to relieve physical or mental stress, to have a good time, to satisfy our impulses, even to prove people "still got it" after a certain age.

Few want to think or talk about the sad thread of pain, suffering, betrayal, lies, broken promises, dysfunctional families, heartache, jaded emotions and mental problems that our nation is reaping as a result of adultery and promiscuity. We can't flaunt God's Word and disregard his warnings and get away with it. Go to our medical wards and count all the sexually transmitted diseases, such as gonorrhea, syphilis, chlamydia (which affects 10 million each year), and AIDS. Have these no bearing on our so-called pleasures?

Today's culture has made sex outside of marriage completely acceptable.

It's troubling to see how adolescents and singles treat sex. God calls it "fornication." They call it "freedom." Today's culture has made sex outside of marriage completely acceptable and, tragically, the norm. Girls go out equipped with condoms or "day after" pills, now that sex has become an expected part of the dating culture. We've set our own rules. But, God's rules haven't changed nor varied. Here are just a few examples:

Acts 15:20: *Write and tell them to abstain from*

eating food offered to idols, from sexual immorality…

1Corinthians 6:18: *Run from sexual sin! No other sin so clearly affects the body as this one does. For sexual immorality is a sin against your own body.*

Galatians 5:19: *When you follow the desires of your sinful nature, the results are very clear: sexual immorality, impurity, lustful pleasures…*

Ephesians 5:3: *Let there be no sexual immorality, impurity, or greed among you. Such sins have no place among God's people.*

Colossians 3:5: *So put to death the sinful, earthly things lurking within you. Have nothing to do with sexual immorality, impurity, lust, and evil desires. Don't be greedy, for a greedy person is an idolater, worshiping the things of this world.*

1Thessalonians 4:3: *God's will is for you to be holy, so stay away from all sexual sin.*

It seems few, however, pay attention to God's Word today. The expectation is for young couples to live together before marriage—a pre-marriage experiment—to make sure they're compatible. That, any way we look at it, is in direct refutation of what God has ordered in His Word.

Adultery reflects an urgent need for help

C. S. Lewis said: "There are people who want to keep our sex instinct inflamed in order to make money out of us. Because, of course, a man with an obsession is a man who has very little sales-resistance." Yes, we all know sex sells. God, on the other hand, wants to nurture our virtues, not our weaknesses. He wants us to look beyond momentary pleasures to those lasting and eternal blessings He's designed for us.

A pastor friend told me about a Prison Fellowship dinner he attended. He sat next to a very elegant lady who looked very out of place in a setting full of former inmates, some of whom were still serving prison sentences. He said he was tempted to ask: "How did an elegant lady like you end up in a place like this?" Instead, he asked: "What is your interest in this organization?"

She looked him straight in the eye and said, "Why, sir, I was a bank robber and murderer. I was in jail and the Lord Jesus reached me through this organization."

My friend said he almost choked on the mouthful of food he'd just put in his mouth. The woman then reached in her purse and pulled out a photograph. "See this picture?" she said. "Do you know who that woman is?"

My friend looked at the picture of a dirty, disheveled, ugly woman with a bitter expression on her face. "No," he answered, "who is she?"

The elegant lady smiled. "That's me," she said. "It was taken the day I was released from prison. The warden gave it to me as a parting present. He told me to take the picture wherever I went so that I'd never forget what I've been."

Like the Prodigal Son, some of us have been

engulfed by terrible sin. We even get to the point of savoring *"the pods that feed the pigs."* It's time, then, to come to our senses and realize that in our father's house there's wonderful food, and enough of it to spare. Who wants to eat pig slop when we could be sitting at God's banquet table? We need to start finding our way back home and leave the pigs and their environment behind.

I remember when I was traveling with Stuart Briscoe in southern Chile, hosting seminars for Spanish pastors. One day we got talking about unusual sermons we'd heard and Ben Haden's name came up—Stuart knew I'd served as Ben's assistant pastor at Key Biscayne.

God wants to nurture our virtues, not our weaknesses.

"Now there's a man who came up with all kinds of surprises," Stuart said. "There's one I'll never forget. For the inauguration of our Elmbrook Church I invited Ben to speak. I was aghast when he got up and started reading his Scripture passage: *"Those who indulge in sexual sin, or who worship idols, or commit adultery, or are male prostitutes, or practice homosexuality, or are thieves, or greedy people, or drunkards, or are abusive, or cheat people—none of these will inherit the Kingdom of God"* (1Corinthians 6:9-10).

"I was embarrassed," Stuart continued, "I wanted to go somewhere and hide. Why would anyone use a reading like that for the inauguration of a church? This was an occasion for joy and celebration, not condemnation. And Ben continued to pour it on. Then he made one of those famous pauses of his and said, 'My friends, I don't know of any part of the Bible that better describes you and me.' I wanted to die," Stuart said, "I'd invited the man. What was I supposed to do, go up and stop him?"

Stuart continued, "At that moment Ben took another one of his long pauses, then said: 'Let's read the next verse: *"Some of you were once like that. But you were cleansed; you were made holy; you were made right with God by calling on the name of the Lord Jesus Christ and by the Spirit of our God"*(1Corinthians 6:11).

"What a sermon!" Briscoe said. "Ben took everything that was bad, perverse and terrible in us and showed us how the Lord had remarkably transformed us into men and women united for the purpose of serving mankind and worshipping God."

By calling on the name of the Lord Jesus Christ and by the Spirit of our God we can be cleansed.

That's exactly the point. Christ wants to transform us. Sinners and adulterers do have an out. There's a great, glorious and effective remedy. By calling on the name of the Lord Jesus Christ and by the Spirit of our God we can be cleansed, we can be made holy and right with God.

On the other hand, if we let our desires and

instincts drive us, God says there will be no salvation. We prove again and again that we have no power. We can't control our appetites and desires. Our sexual impulses easily and quickly overwhelm us. Our only hope is in finding someone powerful enough to save us. That means that only God can do it. We must rely on our powerful Savior for escape. That's the very reason the Lord Jesus asked us to take drastic measures:

> So if your eye—even your good eye—causes you to lust, gouge it out and throw it away. It is better for you to lose one part of your body than for your whole body to be thrown into hell. And if your hand—even your stronger hand—causes you to sin, cut it off and throw it away. It is better for you to lose one part of your body than for your whole body to be thrown into hell (Matthew 5:29-30).

Jesus proposes extreme preventive measures: if your eye betrays you (by what we watch or read), *gouge it out.* In other words, cancel your subscription to *Playboy Magazine;* block pornography from your computers and television sets; refuse to see that provocative new film. Run from the sin that traps you and destroys you. Replace it with decent and uplifting material to read and watch. Like the prodigal, don't you truly want to be free from the pig trough?

I'd like to offer some simple suggestions. Read from the Bible every day and let God's Word speak to you. Spend some time in prayer. Ask for cleansing; ask

God to fill the personal needs of your heart and soul. Pray for God's protection and guidance for your children, relatives, friends, church, and work. In addition, offer to do voluntary work for your church or community. Get involved in something other than yourself. Meanwhile, work with your spouse to fortify your own marriage. Show your love in small ways—flowers, dates, gifts—just as you did when you were dating. Help your spouse with the house chores and ensure that your sexual relationship is solid, tender and satisfying. A healthy marriage can't exist without a healthy relationship.

Seek long-lasting solutions. Our minds have been saturated with illicit thoughts far too long. We need to fill that mental void with positive, godly, useful information. Read uplifting books, those that seriously and carefully deal with biblical concepts, instead of the literary junk that wastes our time. Follow Paul's recommendation in Philippians 4:8: *"Fix your thoughts on what is true, and honorable, and right, and pure, and lovely, and admirable. Think about things that are excellent and worthy of praise."*

The search for forgiveness

I love the story found in John 8. Malicious teachers of Jewish law wanted to catch a woman in the act of adultery in order to trap Jesus into contradicting the laws of Moses.

They spied a woman they saw going into a local

motel with a man who wasn't her husband. At the right moment they bribed the owner to open the door, catching her in the very act of adultery. They dragged the terrified, half-naked woman to the temple where Jesus was teaching. The scene was sadistic, indecent, and vicious. These Pharisees didn't care for the woman, they really didn't care about her sin. All they wanted was to trap Jesus. Just listen to their piety while carrying out their vicious plan:

> Teacher, this woman was caught in the act of adultery. The law of Moses says to stone her. What do you say?

We can imagine the terrified woman waiting for Jesus' condemnation. "What will He say?" she thinks. "Can I stand any more embarrassment?" Imagine being that woman and looking into the eyes of Jesus. But Jesus doesn't say anything. Instead:

> Jesus stooped down and wrote in the dust with his finger. They kept demanding an answer, so he stood up again and said, "All right, but let the one who has never sinned throw the first stone!" Then he stooped down again and wrote in the dust.

The reaction was unexpected. Like pigs wallowing in the mud, each of the accusers slipped away one by one. Now just Jesus and the woman were left. Publicly humiliated, disgraced and disheveled she faces Jesus. She's too ashamed to lift her face. She wants to run, but can't find the strength to leave.

Then Jesus stood up again and said to the woman, "Where are your accusers? Didn't even one of them condemn you?"

She can only muster a whisper: *"No, Lord."*

His response is totally unexpected: *"Neither do I."*

She doesn't know what to say or do. Finally, reluctantly, she begins to walk away. Jesus stops her and gives her a word of godly advice: *"Go and sin no more."*

> Jesus can lift anyone from the misery of sin.

In his confident smile she finds strength. Her clothes are still dirty, but her soul now is clean. She thinks of her husband, of her betrayal. I believe right there and then she makes herself a promise. She'll follow Jesus. She'll work on her marriage. She'll spend the rest of her life pleasing God.

The Bible doesn't reveal her name, but I think she's seen again. I think she's the same woman who entered the home of the Pharisee while Jesus was having dinner (Luke 7:37-48). I think she was the one who wept at his feet, wiping the tears of gratitude off with her hair, then kissing his feet and anointing them with that most expensive of perfumes. When I get to heaven I'm going to ask!

Putting aside such curiosity, the story—and the lesson—is very real. God's forgiveness is amazingly available to those who've fallen. Jesus can lift anyone from the misery of sin with those unbelievable words:

"I don't condemn you. Go and sin no more." It's exactly the same forgiveness King David found after he fell so shamelessly with Bathsheba. It's not that Jesus doesn't care about the gravity of the sin, he forgives because *"he was pierced for our rebellion, crushed for our sins. He was beaten so we could be whole. He was whipped so we could be healed"* (Isaiah 53:5).

God's forgiveness is open, free and accessible. But never forget that it was obtained at the highest possible cost. It's that unthinkable pain he suffered in our place that gives him the right to say, *"I don't condemn you."* At the same time, that inexhaustible forgiveness also brings to us His other insistent demand: *"Go and sin no more."*

THE EIGHTH COMMANDMENT

You must not steal (Exodus 20:15).

Have you ever been robbed?

Have you ever stolen anything?

Imagine a world without thieves.

AMAZINGLY, this commandment, *"You must not steal,"* has been called into question by some people. For example, Ebon Musings (*The Atheism Pages*) doesn't like this commandment at all. He asks: "Can we come up with a new Decalogue that would be more relevant and useful for the world today? The old ten are showing their age and provincial origin by now; we need an updated set."

Of course, practically anyone could come up with ten suggestions, ten principles, or ten regulations. But, can you imagine any re-write that would ever be able to deal as specifically with basic human problems like God's Ten Commandments?

Take as example the problem of thievery and a Department of Commerce study:

- Employee theft and dishonesty cost U.S. business between $60 billion and $120 billion per year ("How to Identify Dishonesty Within Your Business").
- Insider theft is growing at 15% annually (Justice Department).
- Employee theft amounts to 4% of food sales at a cost in excess of $8.5 billion. 75% of inventory shortages are attributed to employee theft (National Restaurant Association).
- Employee theft costs between .5% - .3% of a company's gross sales. Even if the figure is 1%, it still means employees steal over a billion dollars a week from their employers ("How to Identify Dishonesty Within Your Business").
- One third of all employees steal from their employer.

In fact, stealing is so predictable that during the December 2005 refuse worker's strike in New York City, one person cleverly took advantage of it. Needing to get rid of his garbage, he gift wrapped it in a box and left it on the seat of his unlocked car. By evening somebody had stolen it.

The first mention of thievery in the Bible is the story of Jacob stealing his brother Esau's birthright (Genesis 27:31-36):

Esau prepared a delicious meal and brought it to his

father. Then he said, "Sit up, my father, and eat my wild game so you can give me your blessing." But Isaac asked him, "Who are you?" Esau replied, "It's your son, your firstborn son, Esau."

Isaac began to tremble uncontrollably and said, "Then who just served me wild game? I have already eaten it, and I blessed him just before you came. And yes, that blessing must stand!"

When Esau heard his father's words, he let out a loud and bitter cry. "Oh my father, what about me? Bless me, too!" he begged. But Isaac said, "Your brother was here, and he tricked me. He has taken away your blessing."

Esau exclaimed, "No wonder his name is Jacob, for now he has cheated me twice. First he took my rights as the firstborn, and now he has stolen my blessing."

Stealing is condemned throughout the Bible. The last mention is found in Revelation 9:20-21, where it's associated with the most reprehensible of evils:

But the people… still refused to repent of their evil deeds and turn to God. They continued to worship demons and idols made of gold, silver, bronze, stone, and wood—idols that can neither see nor hear nor walk! And they did not repent of their murders or their witchcraft or their sexual immorality or their thefts.

To me, the most dreadful account of a theft and its results is in Joshua 7:19-26, where a Jewish soldier named Achan was found in an act of deliberate disobedience:

> Then Joshua said to Achan, "My son, ...tell me what you have done. Don't hide it from me." Achan replied, "It is true! I have sinned against the LORD, the God of Israel. Among the plunder I saw a beautiful robe from Babylon, 200 silver coins, and a bar of gold weighing more than a pound. I wanted them so much that I took them. They are hidden in the ground beneath my tent, with the silver buried deeper than the rest." So Joshua sent some men to make a search. They ran to the tent and found the stolen goods hidden there, just as Achan had said, with the silver buried beneath the rest. They took the things from the tent and brought them to Joshua and all the Israelites. Then they laid them on the ground in the presence of the LORD... Then Joshua said to Achan, "Why have you brought trouble on us? The LORD will now bring trouble on you." And all the Israelites stoned Achan and his family and burned their bodies. They piled a great heap of stones over Achan, which remains to this day. That is why the place has been called the Valley of Trouble ever since.

In reading and studying the Bible's instructions concerning thievery, I'm impressed by all the respect God gives to other people's property. So important is it, that He's included *you must not steal* as one of His

Ten Commandments. Simply stated, He tells us not to take what belongs to someone else.

This brings us to a short but necessary discussion on the subject of the right to own property. A verse in Acts of the Apostles tells us that *"all the believers were united in heart and mind. And they felt that what they owned was not their own, so they shared everything they had"* (Acts 4:32).

That account seems to imply that the Christian ideal is to share everything one has and not to own anything. Interestingly, it almost appears to endorse the views held by Karl Marx.

Marx called private property the source of all evil and believed that when a person acquired things, the result was always greed—a disposition that ultimately resulted in the exploitation of society. He taught that no one should own anything, everything should be owned by the state. In this way all economic differences would be erased and the world would know equality and justice. Many throughout the world accepted these ideas, and a number of experiments have been attempted to prove Marx's conclusions. One such attempt took place in Latin America in 1892.

I'm impressed by all the respect God gives to other people's property.

An Australian by the name of William Lane— author of the book *The Working Man's Paradise*—set out to create a Marxist paradise. Since Australia—to his way of thinking—was too capitalistic for such a test, he bought 500,000 acres of land from the government of Paraguay. There, bordering the La Plata River, he set out to create a settlement that would overcome the greedy evils of individual ownership and portray the benefits of a Marxist type paradise.

He named his project "The New Australia Cooperative Settlement Association." Many young Australians and socialists were attracted to this concept of equality for all and the absence of capitalism. They joined William Lane in the effort to prove to the world that a successful socialist society could be established, and do it before the end of the 19th century. On July 17, 1893 a ship full of idealists set sail from Sydney, Australia, to their dream paradise in Paraguay.

However, even before the ship reached its destination, problems and arguments developed. Who would be the leader? How would the colony be governed? Lane tried to solve the problem by naming himself governor. After they landed, the disagreements continued. Everyone felt equal. Everyone wanted to do what they felt like doing. The colony became impossible to manage. In his effort to maintain some semblance of order, Lane tried to govern by becoming dictatorial. The colonists rebelled. By December of that very first year, they kicked Lane out.

Determined to save his dream, Lane, along with 45 adults and 12 children, founded another place in Paraguay. This second "paradise" they named Cosme.

In spite of Lane's best efforts, however, families began to abandon the settlement. They couldn't get used to sharing everything. All too many took advantage of the others, creating resentments and jealousies. These, too, came to resent Lane's authoritarianism and, like the first "paradise," this dream also ended in failure. People were simply too selfish to make a socialist community work. In 1899, Lane returned to Australia sick, broke and completely disillusioned.

The positive lesson

Marxism believes that all property belongs to the state, which, in theory, represents all the workers. Capitalism, on the other hand, believes that ownership is the right of every individual. Surprisingly, the Bible rejects both philosophies—we will get to the reasons for that in a moment. First, a brief explanation as to why there's an argument over this issue of property ownership. Many become frustrated because of all the inequality between the haves and the have-nots. The "haves" begin to search for ways to improve society. Their basic concern is the need for justice and equality. They dream of a world that is "fair," where those who have so little are properly protected and cared for.

Social injustice is cruel and vicious. Wherever there are abuses, these should be combated. However, not all inequality is unjust, nor is it necessarily wrong. In fact, inequality isn't only natural, it's inescapable. We're born unequal. Each one of us is born with a different level of capacity, skill and intelligence. God made us all different. To believe that we must all be the same is to go against God's divine plan and design for humanity. On the other hand, every one of us is responsible for what God has given us. Therefore, achieving what we rightfully and honestly can through the use of our gifts and capacities is our God-given duty. We shouldn't despise our abilities nor our opportunities.

The best example is found in the teachings Jesus Himself gave us:

> *Again, the Kingdom of Heaven can be illustrated by the story of a man going on a long trip. He called together his servants and entrusted his money to them while he was gone. He gave five bags of silver to one, two bags of silver to another and one bag of silver to the last—dividing it in proportion to their abilities. He then left on his trip. The servant who received the five bags of silver began to invest the money and earned five more. The servant with two bags of silver also went to work and earned two more. But the servant who received the one bag of silver dug a hole in the ground and hid the master's money* (Matthew 25:14-18).

According to Jesus, whatever we have has been entrusted to us by God. We're duty-bound not only to protect, but to use and invest it. The parable clearly states that some are given more than others. It also shows us that one day we'll all report back to the Giver and explain what we've done with the things entrusted to us:

After a long time their master returned from his trip and called them to give an account of how they had used his money. The servant to whom he had entrusted the five bags of silver came forward with five more and said, 'Master, you gave me five bags of silver to invest, and I have earned five more.' The master was full of praise.

According to Jesus, whatever we have has been entrusted to us by God.

'Well done, my good and faithful servant. You have been faithful in handling this small amount, so now I will give you many more responsibilities. Let's celebrate together! The servant who had received the two bags of silver came forward and said, 'Master, you gave me two bags of silver to invest, and I have earned two more.' The master said, 'Well done, my good and faithful servant. You have been faithful in handling this small amount, so now I will give you many more responsibilities. Let's celebrate together!' Then the servant with the one bag of silver came and said, 'Master, I knew you were a harsh man, harvesting crops you didn't plant and gathering crops you didn't cultivate. I was afraid I would lose your money, so I hid it in the earth. Look, here is your money back.' But the master replied, 'You wicked and lazy servant! If you knew I harvested crops I

didn't plant and gathered crops I didn't cultivate,
why didn't you deposit my money in the bank? At
least I could have gotten some interest on it.' Then he
ordered, 'Take the money from this servant, and give
it to the one with the ten bags of silver. To those who
use well what they are given, even more will be
given, and they will have an abundance. But from
those who do nothing, even what little they have will
be taken away. Now throw this useless servant into
outer darkness, where there will be weeping and
gnashing of teeth (Matthew 25:19-30).

Human law states that we're free to do what we
please and enjoy what is ours. According to what
we've read above, divine law, on the contrary, warns us
that all we have—our money, our house, our business
and our belongings—are on loan to us from God. Each
of us is entrusted by God to properly manage all He's
put in our care. Furthermore, one day He'll call us
to account.

Implications of this commandment

God's intention, then, is that we manage prudently and
wisely whatever He's put in our care. This includes
what we've obtained through honest and pure means.
There are at least five legitimate ways in which God
permits us to acquire things:

1. Through honest and hard work, that is, the work
   of our minds and hands.
2. With the money we earn we're free to purchase

the things we need and want—a home, a car, furniture, and other things we enjoy.

3. Sometimes friends and family have been blessed financially and they wish to share it with others. When we're the recipients, these gifts are proper and good.

4. Inheritances are another way; a close relative designates us as heirs, and leaves us assets or property—a cause for rejoicing.

5. Through good investments. There are many opportunities to invest in legitimate businesses and receive legitimate returns.

In Ephesians 4:28 the Apostle Paul mentions two of these: our work and our donations. He says: *"...use your hands for good hard work, and then give generously to others in need."* Please note the negative implication in that teaching: if we don't work and deliberately remain poor and needy ourselves, our lack of initiative and enterprise means that a key way God has for helping the poor and needy won't take place.

The negative lesson

"You must not steal!" Since, as we've learned, all things belong to God and to steal is to take something God has given to somebody else. Ultimately, then, it means that stealing is taking something that belongs to God.

I recently received a call from the bank where I keep a credit card. They were suspicious about some activity on my account and wanted to confirm that several purchases posted were actually mine. As the bank accountant named each item, I realized someone had indeed stolen my credit card number. Somebody had taken from me that which God had placed in my care. We immediately voided the credit card and the bank, I assume, set out to find out who'd been the thief.

When there's wholesale stealing, and nothing is done to stop it, the integrity of a society is compromised. How can a nation be good and prosperous if it turns a blind eye to fraud, dishonesty, corruption, violations of trust, deceit, false pretenses, unpaid debt and so many other types of theft—big or small? When people steal to get what they want, society as a whole degenerates.

Other kinds of stealing

In the book of Malachi, God asks: *"Should people cheat God? Yet you have cheated me! But you ask, 'What do you mean? When did we ever cheat you?' You have cheated me of the tithes and offerings due to me"* (3:8). Clearly, we cheat God when we deny him the offerings that should be given to His church, and to God Himself. Not to give is tantamount to saying nothing comes from God. I've earned what I have with my efforts, and it belongs to me, I don't care what the Bible says.

But wait a minute! Everything—the air we breathe, the roof over our heads, our food, our clothes, our health, our intelligence, our abilities, and our money—comes from God. We steal directly from God Himself when we take that portion He's asked us to give to Him and use it on ourselves. Further, we can rob God in other ways; for example, when we deny Him the devotion, time, service and love that He deserves as our Maker and King.

Isaiah talks about other ways we steal: *"What sorrow awaits the unjust judges and those who issue unfair laws. They deprive the poor of justice and deny the rights of the needy among my people. They prey on widows and take advantage of orphans"* (10:1-2). Greedy people are quick to steal from the defenseless and the weak, from those who have no voice, no vote, and no protection. Such people, as a result of those abuses, are forced to spend their lives in quiet suffering.

Another way we steal is through gossip and innuendo. When we speak untruth about someone we rob them of the very essence of their being. Unfortunately, it seems as if we enjoy putting others down. That tendency led Benjamin Franklin to say: "To find out a girl's faults, praise her to her girlfriends." How careful we should be when talking about others. I've always liked a saying by George Bernard Shaw: "I like my tailor. He takes my measurements anew each time he sees me, whereas others expect me to fit old measurements." We need to remember that people change, that they learn from their mistakes. Therefore we need to be kind in what we say. When someone comes and speaks ill of a friend, remember the Spanish proverb: "Whoever gossips to you will gossip about you."

In Exodus 22:16 Moses warns about the way

a man can steal a woman's virtue: *"If a man seduces a virgin…and has sex with her…"* the theft involves stealing a woman's innocence. Her reputation, her character and her entire future can be destroyed by such treachery. During ancient times, this crime was punished by making the man pay a significant dowry to the girl's father, or in some circumstances being forced to marry her. Sadly, today this kind of theft is all too often tolerated and even accepted.

Taking another's ideas—or plagiarism—is another way we break the eighth commandment. A pastor friend in Mexico has a large and accessible church. Often he hosts church leaders from different congregations for conferences or prayer meetings. In one of my visits, I noticed he had a big lock and chain around his file cabinet. I asked what this was about and he explained, "Pastors keep stealing my sermons and notes during our meetings. I finally had to lock them up!"

Forgiveness is found when we admit we have a problem we can't fix alone.

I couldn't believe it! Pastors were stealing his sermon notes! They were there to learn, study and pray, but some were there to steal—to try to get ahead by taking someone else's sermons. That still boggles my mind.

How to cure the habit of stealing
We read in Luke 23:41-43 that at His crucifixion Jesus was flanked by two thieves. One hurled insults at

Jesus, but the other said: "We deserve to die for our crimes, but this man hasn't done anything wrong." Turning to Jesus that thief said: *"Remember me when you come into your Kingdom."* Jesus answered: *"I assure you; today you will be with me in paradise."* How wonderful that there's forgiveness for people who steal.

Forgiveness is found, however, when we're ready to admit—like the thief on the cross—that we're guilty and have a problem we can't fix alone. Until we recognize this problem, we'll act like the first thief, despising both the Savior and the Forgiver. But when we understand our weakness, we can go to the One who has the power not only to forgive, but to *"cleanse us from all wickedness"* (1John 1:9). Thank God for such a merciful and powerful Savior!

The second step is given to us by Paul in the advice he gives his disciple Timothy: *"True godliness with contentment is itself great wealth"* (1Timothy 6:6). "Godliness" and "contentment," those are the two key words. They actually summarize everything I've been saying in this chapter. *"Godliness"* is to recognize God as the giver of everything we have, and we love Him for it. *"Contentment"* results from acknowledging that *"the LORD will withhold no good thing from those who do what is right"* (Psalm 84:11).

God, the ruler of heaven and earth, is our gracious and kind caretaker. We rest happily when we understand stealing is not only wrong, but totally unnecessary. He gives and provides us with everything we need.

THE NINTH COMMANDMENT

You must not testify falsely against your neighbor

(Exodus 20:16).

"Do you swear to tell the truth, the whole truth, and nothing but the truth, so help you God?"

Could you truthfully take such an oath?

SOMETIMES it's very difficult to know when someone is telling the truth. Politicians lie to get votes. Salesmen lie to get sales. Coaches lie to get recruits. Even some preachers lie to get offerings. We live in a culture of moral relativism where the truth is shaped by what best suits our purpose.

God gives us the Ninth Commandment to protect the truth. He wants us to tell the truth not only in a court of law, but in every aspect of our lives—no spinning is allowed by Him! In His Word we read, *"Don't lie to each other, for you have stripped off your old sinful nature and all its wicked deeds"* (Colossians 3:9). It seems we pay little regard to this demand. Surveys have shown that 91 percent of us lie every single day—some even more than once. Lying, unfortunately, has become an expected form of communication.

> A lie can generate injustice, distrust, irreparable damage and misery sometimes lasting a lifetime.

Dr. Paul Ekman,[1] who researched the subject of lying for 20 years, says in his book, Telling Lies:

> There are two primary ways to lie: to *conceal* and to *falsify*. In concealing, the liar withholds some information without actually saying anything untrue. In falsifying, an additional step is taken. Not only does the liar withhold true information, but he presents false information as if it were true. Often it is necessary to combine concealing and falsifying to pull off deceit, but sometimes a liar can get away just with concealment… In my definition of a lie or deceit, then, one person intends to mislead another, doing so deliberately, without prior notification of this purpose, and without having been explicitly asked to do so by the target.

Have you ever been told…
• I will love you the rest of my life?

---

[1] Paul Ekman, *Telling Lies: Clues to Deceit in the Marketplace*, Politics, and Marriage, W.W. Norton and Company, p. 28.

THE TEN COMMANDMENTS

- I have never been unfaithful to you?
- I swear I'm not lying?
- I would leave everything I have for you?
- Me, mad at you? What on earth would give you that idea?
- I love you for who you are, not for what you have?
- Of course I forgive you. I don't even remember what you did?
- I'll give you an answer in two words?
- I'll be with you in a second?

Anatomy of a lie

Lies include exaggerations, half truths, false statements, evasion, fallacies, ambiguity, manipulation, inventions, deceit, corruption, misrepresentation, and even the seemingly harmless "white" lies. Proverbs 12:22 says: *"The LORD detests lying lips."* Among the seven things listed in Proverbs 6:16-17 that God hates is *"a lying tongue."*

Lying in many ways is more serious than stealing. Thieves can take away objects that can usually be replaced. A lie, however, can generate injustice, distrust, irreparable damage and misery sometimes lasting a lifetime. That's the reason James admonishes us: *"Don't speak evil against each other, dear brothers and sisters"* (4:11), and John reminds us that outside of heaven are *"the dogs—the sorcerers, the sexually immoral, the murderers, the idol worshipers, and all who love to live a lie"* (Revelation 22:15).

Destructive lies

We have a low opinion of a person who always lies. This is what Solomon said: *"A false witness will not go unpunished, nor will a liar escape"* (Proverbs 19:5). A person, however, who lies to destroy another's character or reputation causes irreparable damage. Remember that Jesus was falsely accused of gluttony, blasphemy, of breaking the law, and even of being possessed by demons. These lies didn't go away; they were repeated again when the Pharisees brought Jesus before Pilate. Even after his crucifixion they continued to lie and discredit him, paying the Roman soldiers guarding his tomb to lie and accusing the disciples of stealing his body.

A pastor friend was forced to leave the ministry after vicious and false accusations were raised against him by a church member. He'd confronted this member of his congregation regarding a grievous sin and, in revenge, this person set out to destroy my friend. Sadly, the lies were spread and believed, and the life and ministry of a man was maliciously destroyed.

Gossips and poisonous tongues are everywhere. As James 3:6-8 says:

> And the tongue is a flame of fire. It is a whole world
> of wickedness, corrupting your entire body. It can set
> your whole life on fire, for it is set on fire by hell
> itself. People can tame all kinds of animals, birds,
> reptiles, and fish, but no one can tame the tongue…It
> is restless and evil, full of deadly poison.

Can lying ever be justified?

Is it ever right to tell a lie? The Bible gives us the story
of Rahab and the lies she told to save the lives of Israeli
spies:

> Then Joshua secretly sent out two spies from the
> Israelite camp at Acacia Grove. He instructed them,
> "Scout out the land on the other side of the Jordan
> River, especially around Jericho." So the two men set
> out and came to the house of a prostitute named
> Rahab and stayed there that night.
>
> But someone told the king of Jericho, "Some Israelites
> have come here tonight to spy out the land." So the
> king of Jericho sent orders to Rahab: "Bring out the
> men who have come into your house, for they have
> come here to spy out the whole land."
>
> Rahab had hidden the two men, but she replied, "Yes,
> the men were here earlier, but I didn't know where
> they were from. They left the town at dusk, as the
> gates were about to close. I don't know where they
> went. [Actually, she had taken them up to the
> roof and hidden them beneath bundles of flax
> she had laid out.] If you hurry, you can probably
> catch up with them." (Joshua 2:1-6)
>
> "Now swear to me by the LORD that you will be
> kind to me and my family since I have helped you.

Give me some guarantee that when Jericho is conquered, you will let me live, along with my father and mother, my brothers and sisters, and all their families."

"We offer our own lives as a guarantee for your safety," the men agreed. "If you don't betray us, we will keep our promise and be kind to you when the LORD gives us the land."

Then, since Rahab's house was built into the town wall, she let them down by a rope through the window (Joshua 2:12-15).

There can be rare circumstances when we'd like to say the truth, but realize that we must hide certain particular things to protect someone's life. There are people in this world who use lies to capture the innocent, torture them and even murder them. We greatly admire Corrie Ten Boom for helping hundreds of Jews escape the Nazis during World War II. Just like Rahab, she had to lie, but her lies saved lives that would've otherwise become victims of Hitler's Holocaust. This leads us to ask: are there circumstances when lying is acceptable under the Ninth Commandment?

The obvious answer is yes, in those rare instances when we're trying to protect someone's life. In such instances lying would be permissible. Other circumstances would be in wartime, when lies are used to confuse and disrupt the enemy. I believe the second half of the Great Commandment allows for such lies, because in this sense we're showing love for our neighbor, just as we'd want someone to lovingly protect us (Matthew 22:39). While our ultimate goal is to do what's right, even in these rare circumstances we're forced to choose the lesser of two evils: telling the truth and causing a life to be destroyed, or telling a lie and saving a life. At the same time we must guard against the idea that "the end justifies the means." That excuse leads to all kinds of mistakes and justifications. Telling a lie, no matter what the reason, is always a sin.

There are people in this world who use lies to capture the innocent, torture them and even murder them.

J.I. Packer[2] says:

> ...a lie as such, however necessary it appears, is bad, not good, and the right-minded man knows this. Rightly will he feel defiled; rightly will he seek fresh cleansing in the blood of Christ, and settle for living the only way one can live with our holy God—by the forgiveness of sins. Again, we say: Lord, have mercy!—and lead us not into this particular type of temptation, where only a choice of sins seems open to us, but deliver us from evil.

---

[2] J.I Packer, *The Ten Commandments*, Tyndale House Publishers, 1982, p. 66

Why we lie

I believe we mostly lie out of pride and convenience. Some people lie so easily and so often they don't even think of telling the truth. Eventually, however, lying catches up to the person and the truth is exposed. People lose all trust in habitual liars, even when they're telling the truth, just like the story of the Shepherd Boy and the Wolf in Aesop's fable.

Jesus tells us: *"Just say a simple, 'Yes, I will,' or 'No, I won't.' Anything beyond this is from the evil one"* (Matthew 5:37). He adds: *"And I tell you this, you must give an account on judgment day for every idle word you speak"* (Matthew 12:36). Paul, in 2Corinthians 12:20, condemns quarreling, slander, and gossip.

Pride makes us lie. We want to appear better than we are, so we exaggerate the truth. Even preachers will at times embellish their sermons with stories that never happened in order to sound more spiritual or more successful. In their desire for recognition some invent having received visions and claim they've received direct revelation from the Lord. Likewise I've heard far too many songwriters claim, "God gave me this song," possibly thinking this add-on will give the song acceptance. However, when the song is played or sung, one would be forced to question both the musicianship as well as the poetry of the "god" who gave it. Because we all want people to recognize and admire us, we easily fall into these traps. The Apostle Paul says: *"I give each of you this warning: Don't think you are better than you really are. Be honest in your evaluation of yourselves, measuring yourselves by the faith God has given us"* (Romans 12:3).

My friend, Stuart Briscoe, says we distort the truth in three ways: through *destructive* lies that aim to hurt others; defensive lies that help us hide something we've done wrong; and *defective lies*, in which we say half-truths to help us hide something. We lie to brag, in order to try to get others to like us; we lie to hide a truth that would otherwise make us look bad and, finally, we stretch the truth to make others believe we're different or better than we really are.

Searching for a cure

Since lying comes so easily, how can we free ourselves from it?

One great truth has helped me: God has never lied and He never will. Many statements in the Bible affirm it: *"God is not a man, so he does not lie"* (Numbers 23:19). *"This truth gives them confidence that they have eternal life, which God—who does not lie—promised them before the world began"* (Titus 1:2). *"He who is the Glory of Israel will not lie"* (1Samuel 15:29). Also, in 1John 1:5 we read: *"This is the message we heard from Jesus and now declare to you: God is light, and there is no darkness in him at all."*

It should go without saying that if I belong to God, if I claim to be His child, I'm to be like Him and follow His example as closely as possible. It's completely unacceptable, then, to be like Jesus and tell lies.

A second thing that's helped me in this area of lying is the statement Paul makes in Ephesians 4:17-25:

> With the Lord's authority I say this: Live no longer as the Gentiles do, for they are hopelessly confused. Their minds are full of darkness; they wander far from the life God gives because they have closed their minds and hardened their hearts against him. They have no sense of shame. They live for lustful pleasure and eagerly practice every kind of impurity. But that isn't what you learned about Christ. Since you have heard about Jesus and have learned the truth that comes from him, throw off your old sinful nature and your former way of life, which is corrupted by lust and deception. Instead, let the Spirit renew your thoughts and attitudes. Put on your new nature, created to be like God—truly righteous and holy. So stop telling lies. Let us tell our neighbors the truth, for we are all parts of the same body.

Jesus has marvelously redeemed me from a world in which lying is acceptable. I don't belong to that world. I belong to the world where truth reigns. I choose to reject lies because those who walk with God are surrounded by truth. This fraternity demands that truth must surround us. Our God is pure truth; there isn't even a shadow of darkness in Him. Those of us who follow Him must seek to reflect the beauty of Christ.

Lies and their consequences

Whenever this subject of lying is discussed, I'm reminded about a lie that was told about my birth.

I was born in Cuba. My father, Elmer Thompson, co-founded a Bible School in the Cuban farmlands, four miles from the city of Placetas, in the geographic center of the island. My mom gave birth to me in a small, two-bedroom wood house with red tiles right in the center of the campus. The house no longer exists; it's an empty lot surrounded by roses. (I've teased my Cuban colleagues, questioning why they haven't built a brass monument in my honor there in that empty lot.)

In any case, my birth was marked by an unmistakable lie told by my father. It happened this way: the campus, called Los Pinos Nuevos (The New Pines) was situated in the municipality of Camajuani—where my father was supposed to register my birth. However, there was no road from Los Pinos Nuevos to Camajuani, and the 15-mile trip had to be made on horseback. Placetas was only four miles away and there was a paved highway right from our Bible School to Placetas. Rather than making the torturous trip to Camajuani, my father decided to register my birth in the municipality of Placetas.

The birth registration representatives asked the normal series of questions to fill out my birth report and my father falsely declared that I'd been born in Placetas. (To top it off, he named me Leslie, a name that's normally given to girls. I won't bother to tell you of the countless telephone calls, correspondence, and medical appointments addressed to Miss Leslie. That's another book!) The point is that my father lied.

"Son," he told me when I was old enough to understand, "God didn't let me get by with that lie. I'd gone to Cuba to train young men to preach God's truth, and here I was lying about my own son's birth. God punished me severely for that lie. After the paperwork was filed, my tongue began to swell. At first I disregarded it as something insignificant, but the swelling increased to the point that I couldn't speak or eat. At that point I had to assume God was punishing me for the lie I'd told about you.

"I struggled with the pain and the swelling for several days, until it became too much to bear. I realized that I'd have to confess my sin to the Cuban officials involved. I took a horse to Camajuani. There, since I couldn't speak, I had to explain the reason for my visit in writing. I asked for forgiveness and then registered your birth. From Camajuani I went back to Placetas and unregistered you. Again, I gave them a written note explaining why, telling them that my ailment was God's punishment for my lie.

"Son, I assure you they were all amazed. They'd never seen a mouth as inflamed as mine, and couldn't believe God would punish someone so severely for telling a lie. Interestingly, the day after I confessed my lies, the swelling went down. The greater reward, however, was that several of the officials who witnessed my confession came to our church in Placetas and heard the Gospel. You can be sure after that experience that I became very conscious of God's demand to always tell the truth."

That lesson has served me, too. Many times, when tempted to tell a lie, I've remembered that story. It's made me fearful of telling lies, and encouraged me to strive to tell the truth. The Apostle Paul, in keeping with the Ninth Commandment, had it right: *"Let everything you say be good and helpful, so that your words will be an encouragement to those who hear them"* (Ephesians 4:29).

THE TENTH COMMANDMENT

You must not covet your neighbor's house. You must not covet your neighbor's wife, male or female servant, ox or donkey, or anything else that belongs to your neighbor (Exodus 20:17).

Ever want something so badly you'd do just about anything to get it?

Is it really fair for some to have so much and others so little?

Could I truly be freed from coveting?

IS IT WRONG to want a two-story house, a good wife, a new car, a successful job, or even a nice summer cottage in the mountains? Not according to this commandment. What would be wrong is to desire your *neighbor's* good wife, your *neighbor's* nice house, new car, job, or air-conditioned house on the beach.

Clearly, the purpose of this commandment is to regulate the area of our desires. It clarifies the distinction between what is legitimately ours (or what we can legitimately obtain), versus what belongs to somebody else.

What the Tenth Commandment censures is the unhealthy, aberrant desire to take things that belong to somebody else; to want something that doesn't belong to you so badly that you'll do just about anything to get it.

The past few commandments warned us against the sinful tendencies related to murder, adultery, stealing and lying. This one explores what goes on in our minds and our thoughts, driving us to plan and plot ways of illegitimately obtaining things that don't rightly belong to us. In the face of our natural tendency to covetousness, our inner struggle has to do with contentment: to learn what Paul was talking about when he said: *"I know how to live on almost nothing or with everything. I have learned the secret of living in every situation, whether it is with a full stomach or empty, with plenty or little"* (Philippians 4:12).

Our inner struggle has to do with contentment.

I'll never forget an incident early in my marriage to Carolyn that could have ended in disaster, all because of a few possessions. So that the story is clear, I need to give a bit of background.

I left Cuba in 1960, after Fidel Castro came to power, and moved to Costa Rica. With me came my assistant Juan Rojas and his wife, Nenita. Juan and I worked at an inter-mission agency called LEAL (Evangelical Literature for Latin America). Like me and so many others who left Cuba, the Rojas' had to leave their homeland with nothing more than the clothes they were wearing, following the rules imposed by Castro's communist regime. Since I was alone, my needs were few (I had lost my first wife during childbirth to our third son and my three children were temporarily staying in Cuba with my missionary brother Allen and his wife). When the Rojas' and I arrived in Costa Rica, our missionary salaries made it very difficult to buy what was needed to set up our new homes.

With that background, let's skip ahead to August of 1962 when I traveled from Costa Rica to Bellingham, Washington, to marry Carolyn. (It still amazes me that this beautiful woman graciously agreed to marry me, along with my three children.) At the wedding we received numerous presents from many kind friends. We packed them in some trunks, stuffed them into the back of a used van and, with our three happy little boys, began our adventurous "honeymoon" journey to San Jose.

I'll skip the part about our adventures on the trip to tell you about our second day in Costa Rica— the day I had my first major conflict with my brand new wife.

I invited Juan and Nenita to our home so they could meet Carolyn. At the same time, I decided it would be a good time to unpack the trunks and get into our wedding presents. Before us were all kinds of things to start a new home: linens, table cloths, plates, silverware, pots and pans, and a fair assortment of kitchen utensils. It was at this moment I got my featherbrained idea. Without any warning (meaning I did not consult with Carolyn), I began dividing up our wedding presents with Juan and Nenita. "This towel is for you, and this one is for us. This tablecloth is for you, this one for us...," without ever glancing up to see Carolyn's eyes filling with tears. In high spirits I went through the entire contents of all the wedding presents.

Needless to say, Juan and Nenita were thrilled. My loving wife, however, was in shock. She couldn't believe what had just taken place before her eyes. No doubt, I was happy about helping the Rojas family, but Carolyn had just met them. Added to that, she was a newlywed in a strange country, with a widower husband and three children, and she didn't know the language Juan, Nenita and I were speaking. She had no idea why I was giving these strangers one half of our things, most of which she was looking at for the very first time. Thinking back, I'm amazed she didn't run out of the house all the way back to Bellingham, as fast as she could.

The second the Rojas's left our house with all "our" stuff, she burst into tears: "What have you done?" she sobbed, "I can't believe you just gave away half of our wedding gifts! You had no right to give away our things without asking me first! How will I ever know how to say thank you?"

Now, years later—and hopefully a bit wiser—I readily acknowledge that my actions were very insensitive and that I acted much like a *macho latino* without regard to my new bride's feelings. I did, however, beg for forgiveness. Then, because I needed her to understand my actions, I took her to see where Juan and Nenita lived. On entering their little run-down apartment and seeing their lack of anything close to the few items we possessed, she did find the mercy and grace to forgive me.

Remembering this incident, I'm reminded how attached we become to things. We become so enamored—even blinded—by what we possess that we simply don't see the bona fide needs of others. Not only do we selfishly grab on to what is ours, we want more and more, even coveting things that belong to others. Sharing with those in need is the furthest thing from our minds.

Contrary to what most people believe, *"Life is not measured by how much you own"* (Luke 12:15). Wise old Solomon in Ecclesiastes 5:10-19 explains:

> *Those who love money will never have enough. How meaningless to think that wealth brings true happiness! The more you have, the more people come to help you spend it. So what good*

is wealth—except perhaps to watch it slip through your fingers!

People who work hard sleep well, whether they eat little or much. But the rich seldom get a good night's sleep.

There is another serious problem I have seen under the sun. Hoarding riches harms the saver. Money is put into risky investments that turn sour, and everything is lost. In the end, there is nothing left to pass on to one's children. We all come to the end of our lives as naked and empty-handed as on the day we were born. We can't take our riches with us.

And this, too, is a very serious problem. People leave this world no better off than when they came. All their hard work is for nothing—like working for the wind. Throughout their lives, they live under a cloud—frustrated, discouraged, and angry.

Even so, I have noticed one thing, at least, that is good. It is good for people to eat, drink, and enjoy their work under the sun during the short life God has given them, and to accept their lot in life. And it is a good thing to receive wealth from God and the good health to enjoy it. To

enjoy your work and accept your lot in life—
this is indeed a gift from God.

Is it wrong to want possessions and financial success?

Let me repeat, wanting things is not a sin. God created us with tremendous potential and powerful desires. There's nothing wrong with wanting a successful business, position, wealth, fame or even a plasma TV. Desire is a natural, God-given instinct. At the same time, as we noted when we studied the Eighth Commandment, our possessions are not really ours. They belong to God. He's made it possible for us to obtain what we have and has charged us with keeping care of it. Psalm 128:2 tells us: *"You will enjoy the fruit of your labor. How joyful and prosperous you will be!"* Likewise, Proverbs 28:20 says: *"The trustworthy person will get a rich reward, but a person who wants quick riches will get into trouble."*

We break the Tenth Commandment when we step across God's boundaries.

We break the Tenth Commandment when we step across God's boundaries. When, to get what we want, we harm our neighbor, steal and take what doesn't belong to us, we clearly violate the Tenth Commandment.

Condorito, a well-known Spanish cartoon character created in Chile, often repeats to his mother, "I'm honest, that's why I'm poor." The idea is that to be rich one has to be dishonest. That's a very mistaken concept and many stories in the Bible disprove it. God made many heroes of our faith very wealthy: Abraham, Isaac, Jacob, Job, David, Solomon, for instance. They all obtained their wealth legitimately, without greed or sinning. For example, we're told that Job was *"blameless, of complete integrity; feared God and stayed away from evil"* (Job 1:1 and 2:3). Job's many possessions came from the blessing of God as a result of his honesty and hard work.

Wishing for success and being gratified by the results of our good, hard work isn't a sin. Remember that when God finished His creation, *"He saw that it was very good"* (Genesis 1:31), and was very satisfied and pleased with every aspect of it. Paul told the Philippians that he worked hard so that *"on the day of Christ's return, I will be proud that I did not run the race in vain and that my work was not useless"* (Philippians 2:16).

I can understand why Paul ran that kind of a race. He was terrified of failure. Actually, who wants to fail? As Christians, we believe "God loves us and has a wonderful plan for our lives." Wishing for success and achieving it, then, is part of our nature; it's not only a gift from God, but proof that we're made in His image.

When God created us He said: *"Be fruitful and multiply. Fill the earth and govern it. Reign over the fish in the sea, the birds in the sky, and all the animals that scurry along the ground"* (Genesis 1:28). God created us to produce, rule, govern and live life to the fullest. The desire to dream, to achieve, to "go for it" comes from God. It's not a sin. It becomes sin when we take those wishes and dreams and try to fulfill them illegitimately, through manipulation, deception, and greed.

What is greed?

In working and struggling for success, have you ever thought of the words Jesus said when introducing the Parable of the Rich Fool, Luke 12:15: *"Beware! Guard against every kind of greed. Life is not measured by how much you own."*

On the other hand, have you ever dreamed about being surrounded by beautiful things, overwhelmed by glorious sounds, savoring the most exotic foods, imagining a very well invested future? Have those kinds of thoughts so filled you with desires that you no longer wanted to hear that still small voice reminding you: *"Life is not measured by how much you own."*?

It's very easy to push God aside when we strive to reach our dreams. Instead of rejoicing in God's blessings and being satisfied with what He gives us, we fill our hearts and minds with all kinds of immoderate and unnecessary wants. WordReference.com explains greed as "reprehensible acquisitiveness; insatiable desire for wealth," or "excessive desire to acquire or possess more (especially more material wealth) than one needs or deserves."

King Ahab (1 Kings 21) serves as an example and

a warning. One day as he traveled around his kingdom, he came across an extraordinarily beautiful vineyard. He marveled at the sight of the bountiful crops, the magnificent gardens, the exquisite fruit trees, and the elegant house. He wanted it. No, he coveted it! He returned to his palace, but couldn't get that farm out of his mind. He talked about its magnificence to his friends, he dreamed about it. And the more he talked and dreamed, the more he wanted it.

He sent his servants to find out who owned it. Discovering it belonged to a man by the name of Naboth, he got into his chariot and went to the man to buy it. But Naboth rejected the king's generous offer, informing him that he loved his farm and nothing would make him sell it. When the king insisted, Naboth explained that all this property had been passed down to him from his ancestors, that it had been the family's inheritance since the days of Joshua. To sell the land would be to betray his ancestors and the God who had so mercifully gifted them with it.

Greed is pandemic. Its tentacles stretch around the world.

King Ahab returned to his palace angry and sullen. He couldn't sleep, he couldn't eat. Like a spoiled child he moped around his palace. That's how Queen Jezebel found him. When she asked what had gotten him so upset, he told her about Naboth's beautiful farm. Once Jezabel learned that a mere commoner was causing the king so much pain, she took the matter into her own hands. She found two scoundrels who for money were willing to lie about Naboth. She then found a corrupt judge who was willing to "believe" those lies. Naboth was summarily put on trial and sentenced to death, and the king and his wicked wife greedily took possession of that which didn't rightfully belong to them.

Note that four of the Ten Commandments were broken: (1) King Ahab *coveted* another's property; (2) the queen got men to give *false testimony*, (3) she found a judge to unjustly *condemn to death* a righteous man; so that (4) they could *steal* property that wasn't theirs. As the prophet Micah said: *"When you want a piece of land, you find a way to seize it. When you want someone's house, you take it by fraud and violence. You cheat a man of his property, stealing his family's inheritance"* (Micah 2:2).

A warning about some religious sects

Greed is pandemic. Its tentacles stretch around the world. Whether on radio or TV, greed seems to high-light most broadcasts. Greed manages to topple the wealthy as well as the poor, to destroy saints as well as scoundrels. 2Peter 2:3 warns that even within the church, there are fraudulent teachers who, *"in their greed they will make up clever lies to get hold of your money."*

I'm reminded of two so called "evangelists" who went to Bogota, Colombia, a few years ago. Twisting the Word of God for their own ends, they promised their gullible Christian audience incredible blessings if they'd give them generous offerings. A person who gave them $100, for example, would soon receive $1,000 from God. $1,000 would grow into $10,000, and the like. They shamelessly declared that God, through them, had come to Bogota, and that God had revealed to them that the more people gave, the greater would be their miraculous rewards. Sadly, people emptied their bank accounts, some refinanced their homes, and others sold their cars. They gave the evangelists their money in hopes of obtaining quick rewards and blessings from God.

Local reporters who witnessed the event began investigating the so called evangelists and discovered a long pattern of fraud and deceit. They reported their findings in the Bogota newspapers, and the two scoundrels fled the country. According to the newspapers, they escaped to Brazil with over two million dollars.

In the Bible we're warned about false prophets. They usually come citing obscure Bible passages and making all kinds of exaggerated promises. Appealing to people's greed, their goal is to steal what doesn't belong to them. On the other hand, true preachers place the teaching of God's truth above financial gain. They teach us to trust in God's ability to fulfill our needs. For example, Matthew 6:33: *"Seek the Kingdom of God above all else, and live righteously, and he will give you everything you need."*

Why God condemns greed

The answer is found in one short sentence: covetousness replaces our confidence in God and places it on ourselves. We covet what others have because we don't believe God can or will provide for us, and we set out to get it ourselves. Greed can actually make us behave like the Israelites did when God sent them manna from heaven (Exodus 16). God promised to give them this miraculous food every day, but most didn't believe it. The first day the manna fell from heaven some went out and gathered as much as they could—just in case. The next morning, when they pulled their manna out of the cupboards, it was full of maggots and had a terrible odor.

We mistakenly assume that we're secure when we work hard and stuff enough away for the future. Deep down we believe our security depends on our personal ability to work and save. It's a strain for us to accept the simple fact Paul gives us: *"This same God who takes care of me will supply all your needs from his glorious riches, which have been given to us in Christ Jesus"* (Philippians 4:19).

Paul adds: *"I have learned how to be content with whatever I have"* (Philippians 4:11). That's the way he conquered his greed. There's great contentment when from our hearts we trust in God's promises, when we understand that God provides exactly what each of us needs. That's the kind of trust that believes the truth of Hebrews 13:5: *"God has said, 'I will never fail you. I will never abandon you.'"*

Faith and greed cannot coexist. When we covet, it's because we no longer are willing to believe in God's power to provide. We don't believe the promise made us by Jesus:

> *So don't worry about these things, saying, 'What will we eat? What will we drink? What will we wear?' These things dominate the thoughts of unbelievers, but your heavenly Father already knows all your needs. Seek the Kingdom of God above all else, and live righteously, and he will give you everything you need* (Matthew 6:31-33).

Some concluding thoughts

To be infected by covetousness doesn't mean a person has to be rich or powerful. Some of the most covetous people in the world are very poor, as are some of the richest. Newspapers constantly carry stories about the lies, thefts, and murders committed on account of greed. The stories confirm these acts are committed by both the rich and the poor. 1Timothy 6:10 explains it: *"For the love of money is the root of all kinds of evil. And some people, craving money, have wandered from the true faith and pierced themselves with many sorrows."*

In our world today, it seems every possible wish is being expertly promoted and advertised. Much of advertising is playing on our greed. The ads make us believe our life is incomplete and miserable unless we get what they're promoting. This is the very reason we must learn to distinguish between wants and needs.

Our ancestors managed to have great, rewarding, and successful lives without cars, cellular phones, wide-screen television sets, and even electricity. Today, for instance, most of us can't imagine life without a car. The problem is we don't want an ordinary car, we want a Lamborghini.

I was in Cuba a few years ago visiting the house where I lived with my family during my ten years of ministry there. Everything seemed so small. The rooms had barely enough space to fit a bed. Back then the tiny living room was furnished with a few chairs because we couldn't afford a sofa. The kitchen had one small cabinet, but it was more than enough for the few things we had.

When we covet, it's because we no longer are willing to believe in God's power to provide.

Actually, I had forgotten all about the house and its lacks. What I remembered most about those ten years was how happy we were. Now, as I walked around the place, I couldn't help but wonder about the many things that so easily complicate our lives today—so much of it a consequence of greed. We've come to believe that if we buy the right stuff, if we get more and bigger and better and more expensive things, then we'll be happy. Socrates was right when he said, "He who is not contented with what he has, would not be contented with what he would like to have."

God in His Word faithfully gives us an answer for all our greed:

> *True godliness with contentment is itself great*
> *wealth. After all, we brought nothing with us*
> *when we came into the world, and we can't take*
> *anything with us when we leave it. So if we have*
> *enough food and clothing, let us be content. But*
> *people who long to be rich fall into temptation and*
> *are trapped by many foolish and harmful desires*
> *that plunge them into ruin and destruction.*
> (1 Timothy 6:6-9).

Happiness does not come through possessions or personal achievements; it's a byproduct of contentment. When Paul made his statements about contentment to the Philippian Christians he was a prisoner shut up in Nero's dungeon at Rome. One wonders how he could possible be content under those circumstances. Was it not because he'd learned that a good, perfect, and loving God was in total control of every circumstance? When a person rests in that knowledge, then, like Paul, he can relax.

The acceptance of our God-given circumstances doesn't mean we no longer pursue goals or desire improvement. It simply means our trust in God releases us from feeling we're lacking something. Neither is it a matter of complacency. It simply means that we see all the God-given good that surrounds us and our craving for things to be different vanishes. We've learned that *"whatever is good and perfect comes down to us from God our Father"* (James 1:17). Our satisfaction is in Him. He's become the wonderful answer to our problem of greed.

Epilogue

AN INTERESTING article in *Time Magazine*[1] reports that thousands of non-Arabs are converting to Islam—even some evangelicals. Allegedly, many of the converts are young Christians who have been seeking solid answers to questions they feel have been ignored by Christianity. In particular, they want answers to the growing wave of uncontrolled sex, violence, and the endless extravagance that has taken over modern society.

While the reasons for converting vary widely, the article cites one common denominator among the young converts: "In an increasingly secular world in which society's rules get looser by the day, Islam provides a detailed moral map covering everything from friendships to protecting the environment." One example is Don Stewart-Whyte, who changed his name to Abdul Waheed, and converted in 2006 to give up his drug and alcohol addictions. He grew a beard and now wears the traditional Islamic dress. Another is Brian Young who converted to Islam as an answer to the decadence of Western society.

"Islam is a kind of refuge for those who are downtrodden and disenfranchised because it has become the religion of the oppressed," says Farhad Khosrokhavar, a Paris professor and author of several books on Muslim extremism. "Previously—say 20 years ago—they may

---

[1] *TIME Magazine*, August 28, 2006, "Allah's Recruits: why more and more westerners are converting to Islam and, in some cases pursuing an extremist path", p. 36.

have chosen communism or gone to leftist ideologies. Now Islam is the religion of those who fight against imperialism, who are treated unjustly by the arrogant Western societies and so on."

I find this shocking. Is Islam with the Koran clearer than the Bible in addressing the problems and needs of humanity? Of course not. The truth is that there is no comparison between the two faiths. Those who seek fair and inclusive laws to achieve a society with high ideals need only look at the books of Exodus, Leviticus, and Deuteronomy. The Koran pales in comparison. Throughout the history of law there has not been a broader and more satisfactory summary of human conduct and requirements than what is found in the Ten Commandments. God has clearly told all of us how to behave.

We can find fair and inclusive laws to achieve a society with high ideals in the books of Exodus, Leviticus, and Deuteronomy.

I can only assume that these young men have searched for answers in the Koran because they never truly studied the Bible, let alone the Ten Commandments. They didn't discover that the Bible contains the most fair, clear and extensive laws to do with human conduct, all wrapped around grace, love and pure justice.

I do believe, however, that far too often as an evangelical community we have failed Christianity by not living up to the standards God has so graciously given us. We have failed to teach and live by these divine principles in our homes, churches, schools and our society. We need to practice what God solemnly requested in Deuteronomy 6:6-9:

> And you must commit yourselves wholeheartedly to these commands that I am giving you today. Repeat them again and again to your children. Talk about them when you are at home and when you are on the road, when you are going to bed and when you are getting up. Tie them to your hands and wear them on your forehead as reminders. Write them on the doorposts of your house and on your gates.

Clearly, those who turn their backs on Christianity don't do so because it lacks clear or specific laws. In this short book I have tried to show that the most important and fair laws known to humanity are abundantly clear in the Ten Commandments. We must live according to these mandates, and we must teach them—not as the way to salvation, because that road is only in our Savior Jesus Christ—but as principles of honesty and proper behavior that God our father expects of us. Only then will we have homes, churches, societies and nations that love God with all their hearts, souls and minds, and love their neighbors as they love themselves.

Now, one final suggestion: please go back and reread the foreword to this book, to remind yourself of the purpose of the Ten Commandments.